Uses the Latest Nutritional Guidelines and Exchanges

Everyday Cooking for Diabetics

Over 200 delicious, specially created recipes

which provide healthy, balanced meals

suitable for the entire family

STELLA BOWLING

FISHER *er* BOOKS™

Acknowledgments

I would like to thank my colleagues for making this book possible, and particularly Anita Ryan for her invaluable help in typing the manuscript.

The most thanks go to my husband Karl for his encouragement and patience, as well as his constructive comments. Thanks also to my nieces Katie and Amy Hancock and my cousin Emma Thomas for their tasting skills and comments. And last but not least, thanks to my baby daughter Jade for sleeping enough in her early weeks to allow me time to test the recipes!

Publishers: Bill Fisher, Howard Fisher, Helen V. Fisher

Managing Editor: Sarah Trotta
North American Editors: Jeanette Egan, Helen V. Fisher
Cover design: FifthStreetdesign
Book design: Deanie Wood
Book production: Randy Schultz, Deanie Wood
Illustrations: Madeline David
Photography: Tim Imrie
Food Styling: Anne Dolamore

First published by Grub Street, London, England
Text copyright ©1995 British Diabetic Association
Copyright ©1995 Grub Street, London
Photographs ©1995 Grub Street, London

North American edition
Published by Fisher Books
4239 W. Ina Road, Suite 101
Tucson, AZ 85741
(520) 744-6110

©1997 Fisher Books
Printed in USA
Printing 10 9 8 7 6 5 4 3 2

Library of Congress Cataloging-in Publication Data

Bowling, Stella, 1962- (Everyday diabetic cookbook)
Everyday cooking for diabetics / Stella Bowling.
p. cm.
Published in the United Kingdom under the title: Everyday diabetic cookbook.
Includes index.
ISBN 1-55561-118-4
1. Diabetes--Diet therapy --Recipes. I. Title.
RC662.B686 1997   616.4' 620654--dc21   96-47314   CIP

Contents

Preface

Food and eating are part of life's great pleasures. Diabetes need not change that. Today, people with diabetes are advised to eat a wide variety of healthful foods and nothing is completely taboo.

As you will see from this book, the diet for people with diabetes is the same as the diet recommended for everyone who is interested in healthful eating—high in fiber, low in fat and low in sugar.

This cookbook shows you how easy eating healthfully can be. It also shows you that following the dietary guidelines does not mean that food is less enjoyable. Neither does it mean that you give up all your favorite foods completely or have less pleasure from interesting meals and new recipes. What is important is eating a balanced diet with a wide variety of foods and having an increased awareness of which foods promote good health, and which foods should be eaten only in moderation.

Everyday Cooking for Diabetics provides a wide range of recipes to help you put the dietary recommendations for diabetes into practice. But, before you start cooking, we will look at diabetes in more detail and explore the background of the dietary recommendations.

Diabetes
and a Healthful
Lifestyle

What Is Diabetes?

Diabetes or, to use its full name, *diabetes mellitus*, is a common condition in which the amount of *glucose* (sugar) in the blood is too high. The body can't use it properly because the body is not converting glucose into energy as it should. Normally the amount of glucose in our blood is carefully controlled by a hormone called *insulin*. Insulin is made by a gland called the *pancreas*, which lies just behind the stomach. Insulin helps glucose enter the cells, where it is used as fuel.

We obtain glucose from the food that we eat, either from sweet foods or from the digestion of starchy foods, such as bread or potatoes. Glucose can also be made by the liver. After a meal, the blood-glucose level rises and insulin is released into the blood. When the blood-glucose level falls (for example, during exercise), the insulin level falls, too. Insulin plays a vital role in regulating the body's blood-glucose level and, in particular, in preventing the blood-glucose level from rising too high.

There are two main types of diabetes: Insulin-dependent diabetes mellitus,or IDDM (also known as *Type* I *diabetes*) and non-insulin-dependent diabetes mellitus, or NIDDM (also known as *Type* II *diabetes*).

Insulin-dependent Diabetes Mellitus (IDDM)

Insulin-dependent diabetes develops when there is a severe lack of insulin in the body because most or all of the pancreatic cells that produce it have been destroyed. This type of diabetes usually appears in people under the age of 40, often in childhood. As mentioned earlier, insulin-dependent diabetes develops when the insulin-producing cells in the pancreas have been destroyed. Nobody knows for sure why these cells are damaged. The most likely cause is an abnormal reaction of the body against the cells. This may be triggered by a viral or other infection. Both sexes are equally affected. It is treated by insulin injections and diet.

Non-insulin-dependent Diabetes Mellitus (NIDDM)

Non-insulin-dependent diabetes mellitus develops when the body can still produce some insulin, though not enough for its needs, or when the insulin that the body does produce is not working properly. This type of diabetes usually appears in middle-age or elderly people who are older than 40. It appears occasionally in younger people. It used to be called *adult-onset diabetes*. It is treated by diet alone and tablets or occasionally by diet and insulin injections.

In most cases, the body no longer responds normally to its own insulin. Overweight people are particularly likely to develop NIDDM. The condition tends to run in families and is more common in sections of the Asian community. Some people wrongly describe this as "mild" diabetes. All diabetes should be taken seriously and treated properly.

There are other causes of Type II diabetes, but they are very rare. They include certain diseases of the pancreas. Sometimes, an accident or an illness may reveal the presence of diabetes, but these events do not cause it.

What are the symptoms of diabetes?

The main symptoms of diabetes are:

- thirst and a dry mouth
- passing large amounts of urine (especially during the night)
- tiredness
- blurred vision
- weight loss
- genital itching

Non-insulin-dependent diabetes develops slowly and the symptoms are usually less severe. Some people may not notice any symptoms at all but their diabetes is discovered in a routine medical checkup. People sometimes mistakenly attribute the symptoms to "getting older" or "overwork." Insulin-dependent diabetes develops much more quickly, usually over a few weeks. In both types, the symptoms are quickly relieved once the diabetes is treated.

WHO GETS DIABETES AND WHAT CAUSES IT?

Diabetes is a common health condition. In the United States, about 8 million people are known to have diabetes. For every person who knows that he or she has it, there is probably another person with diabetes who doesn't realize it. Over three-quarters of people with diabetes have the non-insulin-dependent type. Diabetes can occur at any age, but it is rare in infants.

Diabetes is not caused by eating sweets or the wrong kind of food. Stress does not cause diabetes either, although it may make the symptoms worse if diabetes is already present. You cannot catch diabetes from somebody, nor can you give it to others.

HOW IS DIABETES TREATED?

Although diabetes cannot be cured, it can be treated successfully. Before discussing the different kinds of treatment, it is important to know how diabetes affects blood-glucose levels.

When carbohydrates (sugary and starchy foods) are digested, they turn into glucose. As we have seen, people with diabetes are unable to turn glucose into energy the body needs. There is not enough insulin available for that process to take place (or available insulin is not used properly). In response, the liver makes more glucose than usual, in an effort to make more energy available. However, the extra glucose cannot be turned into energy, either. The body breaks down its stores of fat and protein next, to try to release more glucose—but that glucose also cannot be turned into energy. This process explains why people with untreated diabetes often feel tired and lose weight. Finally, the unused glucose spills over into the urine for elimination, which is why people with untreated diabetes need to urinate more often.

Insulin-dependent diabetes is treated by injections of insulin and a healthful diet. Non-insulin-dependent diabetes is treated by a healthful diet or by the combination of a healthful diet and drugs. Sometimes people with non-insulin-dependent diabetes also take insulin injections, but they are not totally dependent on the injections.

Insulin-dependent Diabetes

People with insulin-dependent diabetes need to take injections of insulin for the rest of their lives. They also need to eat a healthful diet that contains the right balance of foods. Insulin cannot be taken by mouth in the way medicines can because it is destroyed by the digestive juices in the stomach. A flexible regimen with up to four insulin injections each day may be used.

If you or someone close to you needs to take insulin injections, your doctor or diabetes nurse will talk to you, show you how to do them and give you all the support and help you need. They will also show you how you can do a simple blood or urine test at home to measure your glucose levels so that you can adjust your insulin and diet according to your daily routine. They will advise what to do if your glucose level is too low. If you have this type of diabetes, insulin injections are necessary to keep you alive. You must take them every day.

Non-insulin-dependent Diabetes

People with non-insulin-dependent diabetes need to eat a healthful diet that contains the right balance of foods. If your doctor or diabetes nurse finds that diet alone is not enough to keep your blood-glucose levels normal, you may be given tablets to take. There are two types of diabetes tablets. One type helps your pancreas produce more insulin. The other type helps your body make use of the insulin that your pancreas is producing. Sometimes a combination of tablets is prescribed. Your doctor or diabetes specialist will tell you all about the tablets, including when to take them and how to monitor your blood- or urine-glucose levels.

HEALTHFUL EATING

What you eat directly affects your blood-glucose levels. It can also influence the amount of fat (such as cholesterol) in your blood. It is important to eat the right kinds of foods to stay healthy. The diet recommended for people with diabetes is not a "special" diet. It is the same kind of healthful eating plan that is recommended for *everybody*—high in fiber and low in sugar and fat.

Guidelines for Diabetes

- Eat regular meals and try to eat similar amounts of carbohydrates from day to day. Follow your physician's and dietitian's advice.
- Base meals on high-fiber carbohydrate foods. The fiber in beans, peas, lentils, vegetables, fruit and oats is particularly good.
- Cut down on fried and fatty foods such as butter, margarine, fatty meat and cheese. Control your fat intake, particularly saturated fats.
- Reduce your sugar intake by cutting down on high-sugar foods and drinks.
- Aim to get to the weight that is right for you and stay there.
- Be careful not to use too much salt.
- Cut down on alcohol and never drink on an empty stomach.
- Avoid special diabetic food and drink products. They are expensive and offer no special benefit.

You don't need special foods because you have diabetes. You may be advised to change the way you cook some foods, alter some ingredients in your recipes (for example, by using a different fat or oil), or to eat less of certain foods. However, the basic foods themselves will mostly be those that you have always eaten.

No one can be expected to make drastic dietary changes overnight. Instead, make the changes gradually—one or two changes a week. You will soon find that you are eating healthful, balanced meals every day that are enjoyable, too! For example, if you need to cut down on fat in your diet, you could substitute a lowfat spread or soft margarine in place of hard margarine or butter one week, and then change from using whole milk to skim or lowfat in the following weeks. Here are the recommendations in more detail:

Eat regular meals. Our bodies prefer to have a regular supply of food. This preference has the advantage of helping to keep blood-sugar levels steady. Try to eat three meals a day; if you don't usually like to eat breakfast, try having a couple of pieces of toast mid-morning instead.

Eat small snacks between meals. You may have been advised by your dietitian to do this, because well-timed snacks can prevent your blood-sugar level from falling too low before your next meal is due. Good choices for snacks include bread (such as a sandwich), plain cookies, cereals or fruit.

Enjoy your food! This is important. All foods can provide some nutrients and add variety to your eating plan, but some foods (such as very sugary foods or drinks) should not be eaten too often or in large quantities if you want to ensure good blood-glucose control.

Eat a variety of foods. Variety is an important factor, because no single food contains all the nutrients your body needs in the required amounts. You have to eat a mixture of foods to get the right amount of nutrients. This is easier to do if you choose foods from each of the four main food groups each day—starchy foods; dairy products; meat, poultry, fish and alternatives; vegetables and fruit.

EAT HIGH-FIBER CARBOHYDRATE FOODS

Many people believe that people with diabetes have to cut down on starchy-carbohydrate foods such as bread, potatoes, pasta, rice and tortillas, but this is not true. By eating plenty of these high-carbohydrate, high-fiber foods as part of a generally healthful and varied diet, your blood-sugar control may improve. Ideally, starchy-carbohydrate foods should form the main part of your meal. Meat, fish or cheese (that is, the protein foods), should be the smaller part. A simple way of ensuring this is to let the starchy component of your meal fill half your plate.

Hints

Eat some starchy-carbohydrate food at every meal. Examples include bread, breakfast cereals, tortillas, noodles, pasta, potatoes, rice, plantains and green bananas. Make these foods the main part of your meal.

Eat roughly the same amounts of carbohydrates from day to day.

Fiber

Fiber is simply the part of food that you don't digest. It used to be referred to as *roughage*. Fiber helps maintain a healthy digestive system and reduces the risks of developing bowel disorders, such as diverticulitis and hemorrhoids. It also helps prevent constipation and colon cancer.

Fiber is found in a wide range of foods, such as whole-grain breads, vegetables, fruit, whole-wheat breakfast cereals, whole-wheat pasta, lentils and beans. Animal products such as meat, cheese or eggs do not contain fiber.

The type of fiber found in fruit and vegetables, beans, lentils and oats is referred to as *soluble fiber* and is particularly beneficial. Soluble fiber helps control blood-glucose levels by slowing down the rate at which sugars in food get into the blood. It also appears to lower cholesterol levels in the blood.

High-fiber carbohydrate foods can help control your weight because they are filling without providing too many calories, and they take longer to eat. Many people believe that starchy foods such as bread, pasta, potatoes, noodles and rice are particularly fattening. This is not true, but they can become high-calorie if served or cooked with fat (for example, potatoes cooked in fat to make French fries, or bread spread with a lot of butter or margarine). Whole-grain varieties of starchy foods are a particularly good choice; whole-wheat bread, brown rice and whole-wheat pasta are good examples. These choices are richer in soluble fiber, contain more vitamins and minerals, and are more filling than the ordinary varieties. Adding bran to foods to increase your fiber intake is not generally recommended, because bran does not provide the nutrients found in foods that are naturally high in fiber.

You will need to drink more fluid when you increase the amount of fiber in your diet. Drink at least 6 to 8 cups of water each day. Increase the amount of fiber in your diet gradually, because it may upset your digestive system if you suddenly consume more fiber than your body is used to.

Hints to Increase Fiber in Your Diet

Choose whole-grain bread, whole-wheat pitas or tortillas rather than white bread, or try a high-fiber white bread. Choose whole-grain or high-fiber breakfast cereals and preferably those without sugar. Good choices include bran cereals and oatmeal. Try using whole-wheat flour in baking instead of white flour, or try using half whole-wheat and half white flour.

Eat whole grains, such as brown rice. Brown rice requires a longer cooking time and more water than white rice, but it has the advantage of not clumping together as easily as white rice. Many people find it tastier.

Try dishes based on pasta, particularly whole-wheat pasta. For example, try Spaghetti Bolognese as the Italians eat it—lots of pasta with just a *little* meat sauce. Try the recipe in this book, which has a lower fat content than ordinary Bolognese recipes.

Eat at least 5 servings of fruit and vegetables (not including potatoes) each day. As well as providing soluble fiber, fruits and vegetables contain the antioxidant vitamins C, E and beta carotene, which may protect against heart disease.

Eat plenty of fruit, vegetables and legumes such as peas, beans and lentils. These are particularly good sources of soluble fiber. Beans and lentils are also a good, lowfat source of protein.

Use more peas, beans and lentils in recipes. In many dishes you can replace some or all of the meat with beans. Try adding lentils to soups, casseroles and other dishes you make. They are more economical, too.

A wide selection of canned beans is available, including kidney beans, chickpeas and nonfat refried beans. Canned beans are easy to prepare and, unlike dried beans, do not require soaking overnight. If you use dried beans, make sure they are cooked properly, following the package instructions. Dried beans should be boiled for 10 minutes, then simmered until soft. Most require soaking for a few hours or overnight.

CONTROL AMOUNTS OF SUGAR

You don't have to cut out sugar completely when you are diagnosed with diabetes. The latest studies show that sugar (*sucrose*) affects blood-sugar levels the same way that starchy carbohydrates do. Sugar can be part of an overall healthful-eating plan, but use it in moderation. It is a good idea to limit the amounts of foods you eat that are high in sugar, such as candies and soft drinks. Also, desserts should be limited because they are high in fat and low in other nutrients.

You can bake your own desserts, such as cakes or sweet breads, and control the amount of fat and sugar used. The amount of sugar in the recipes you use can often be reduced by one-third to one-half with acceptable results. Because sugar affects the browning and texture as well as the flavor of a baked product, it is difficult to eliminate sugar completely in baking. Read the advice on pages 23-24 for adapting your own favorite recipes. Or try the tested reduced-sugar recipes in this book.

Apart from the effect sugary foods have on diabetes control, another reason to limit these foods is tooth decay. Eating sugar is the main cause of tooth decay, especially when sugary foods and drinks are eaten frequently throughout the day. Too much sugar in the diet may also contribute to a general excess of energy (calories), which in turn causes obesity. If you are overweight, cutting down on sugar is one of the easiest ways to reduce calories without losing valuable nutrients.

Hints for Eating Less Sugar

- Cut down on very sugary foods such as sweets and chocolates. Save these for special occasions and preferably eat them after a meal.
- Try drinking tea and coffee without sugar. If you are used to having a lot of sugar in drinks, you may find it easier to cut down a little at a time. If you can't get used to drinks without sweetness, try using an artificial sweetener.
- Use an artificial sweetener instead of sugar to sweeten breakfast cereals, milk puddings or custard and sweet sauces.
- When buying soft drinks, choose low-calorie or diet drinks, rather than the regular versions sweetened with sugar.
- Read the labels on food and watch out for hidden sugar. Flavored lowfat yogurts, for example, can be high in sugar. Choose those sweetened with an artificial sweetener instead.

- Choose low-sugar or sugar-free desserts, such as canned fruit in juice rather than syrup, sugar-free dessert toppings or sugar-free gelatin desserts.
- Use less sugar in baking. The recipes and advice in this book will give you ideas for adapting your own recipes.
- The table that follows gives you some low-sugar or sugar-free alternatives to high-sugar foods.

Artificial Sweeteners

Artificial sweeteners provide an intense level of sweetness when only a minute quantity is used. They can be sprinkled on cereals, stewed fruit or in hot and cold drinks without adding carbohydrate or calories. They are also found in manufactured products such as sugar-free desserts, diet yogurts, sugar-free chewing gum, carbonated diet drinks and low-calorie juice drinks. Artificial sweeteners are available in different forms—tablets, granules or liquid. They have different tastes and sweetening capacities, so you will probably find a brand that suits your particular needs.

Unfortunately, artificial sweeteners are not suitable for many baking purposes. No variety of artificial sweetener can be used when caramelizing or for meringues. They do not trap air as sugar does, so you have to adapt the recipe you are using—even for those varieties of artificial sweetener that are suitable for baking. You may have to incorporate additional air into the mixture by other means, such as sifting flour or beating for a longer time. Expect the baked volume of a cake made with a saccharin-based sweetener to be much smaller than if it were baked with a reduced amount of sugar.

The names of the commonly available sweeteners are: saccharin, aspartame and acesulfame K. Brand names are on page 10.

Which Sweeteners Are Suitable for Baking?

Sweeteners based on aspartame are not suitable for cooking and baking. Aspartame breaks down at prolonged high temperatures and loses its sweetness. Aspartame-based sweeteners are best used when they can be added *after* the cooking process. Examples are custards, stewed fruit, puddings or cold desserts. They are also ideal for sprinkling on foods such as breakfast cereals.

You may heat saccharin-based sweeteners. The granulated or liquid forms can replace sugar in baking recipes, such as scones, quick breads and pies. Other uses include puddings, stewed fruits, fruit pies and some cakes and cookies. Like aspartame-based sweeteners, they are also suitable for sweetening cold desserts, such as mousses and cheesecakes.

Acesulfame K sweetners can be used for baking, as well as in cold desserts.

Alternatives to High-sugar Foods

High-sugar Foods	Low-sugar or Sugar-free Alternatives
Sugar	Have tea or coffee without sugar or use an artificial sweetener
Regular carbonated and other soft drinks	Sugar-free soft drinks Lemonade or juice drinks Diet drinks or sparkling water
Canned fruit in syrup	Canned fruit in natural juices or water
Fruit yogurts	Diet yogurts
Jam, marmalade, honey	Reduced-sugar jams and marmalades, all-fruit spreads
Desserts	Low-sugar rice pudding (canned or made with skim milk and a sweetener). Sugar-free dessert toppings, fresh fruit, sugar-free gelatin desserts or cooked fruit
Filled or frosted cookies	Plain cookies such as vanilla wafers, graham crackers or gingersnaps
Candies	Fresh fruit for snacks
Hot chocolate	Low-calorie chocolate drinks
Rich cakes	Angel-food cakes or unfrosted plain cakes

Sweeteners

Aspartame	Saccharin	Acesulfame K
Equal®	SugarTwin®	Sweet One®
Nutra-Sweet®	Sweet & Low®	
	Sprinkle Sweet®	

How Much Sweetener Is Needed?

Some granulated sweeteners contain bulking agents that enable them to be used spoon-for-spoon like sugar. For example, one teaspoon of sugar would be replaced by one teaspoon of granulated sweetener. Follow the instructions on the package.

Liquid sweeteners are very intense and 8 to 10 drops equal a teaspoon of sugar. One teaspoon of a liquid sweetener generally provides the same degree of sweetness as 10 teaspoons of sugar.

Tablet sweeteners are best used for sweetening hot or cold drinks and are not generally used for baking. Each tablet has the sweetening strength of 1 teaspoon of sugar. So if you usually have 2 teaspoons of sugar in a cup of coffee, you would use about 2 tablets to get the same sweetness.

Eat Less Fat

A small amount of fat in the diet is essential for health and makes food more pleasant to eat. However, most of us eat far more fat than necessary. People with diabetes have a greater risk of developing coronary heart disease, and eating less saturated fat is a major factor in reducing that risk. High-fat foods also tend to be high in calories, so cutting back on them also helps you control your weight.

Types of Fat

There are two main types of fat in foods, *saturated* and *unsaturated*. Foods that are high in saturated fats tend to be animal products, such as butter, lard, fatty meat and full-fat dairy products (such as cheese and milk). These foods should only be eaten in moderation. Saturated fats tend to raise the cholesterol in blood, increasing the risk of heart disease.

Unsaturated fats include *polyunsaturated fats* and *monounsaturated fats*. These fats are thought not to raise the cholesterol in blood and therefore may help to protect against heart disease. Polyunsaturated fats are found in oily fish such as herring, mackerel, tuna and sardines; corn oil, sunflower, safflower and soybean oil; and soft margarines or spreads. Sources of monounsaturated fats include olive, canola and peanut oils.

Hints to Reduce Fat

- Choose a lowfat or reduced-fat vegetable-oil spread or soft margarine rather than butter or hard margarine. If you do use a reduced-fat spread, don't put on more because it's lower in fat!
- If you want to continue using butter, spread it very thinly.
- Try not using any spread sometimes or try having bread the European way—very fresh, with no butter or margarine.
- Use lowfat and skim milk instead of whole milk. Skim milk has a more watery taste and may take longer to get used to. Both lowfat and skim

milks have just as much calcium and protein as whole milk, but have much less fat and calories. Try using them in cooking and for drinks and cereals.

- Try lowfat or fat-free plain yogurt or fat-free sour cream instead of cream for some dishes. If you do use cream, use less or choose a reduced-fat version.
- Cut down on cheese, or replace full-fat hard cheese with reduced-fat or lowfat versions. Try cottage cheese or ricotta cheese in place of full-fat cream cheese. Fat-free cream cheese is available.
- Eat cakes, cookies and pastries in moderation; they are generally high in fat and calories.
- Eat fish instead of fatty meat more often. Oily fish, such as herring, mackerel and sardines, are particularly good choices. Grill, microwave, steam or bake fish rather than deep-frying in batter.
- Buy the leanest cuts of meat you can afford and trim off all the visible fat. Use less meat in recipes and replace or mix it with vegetables, or legumes such as beans or lentils.
- Remove skin from chicken and turkey before eating. Most of the fat is found just under the skin and is easily removed with it.
- Cut down on meat products such as sausages, bacon, hamburgers and hot dogs that are high in fat. Grill hamburgers and sausages rather than frying them.
- Cut down on French fries or use reduced-fat, oven-baked French fries instead.
- Use a rack when roasting meat so the fat drains off the roast and into the roasting pan.

Ways to Reduce Fat

Changing the way you cook can help you cut down on added and unnecessary fat in your diet.

- Measure oil with a tablespoon rather than pouring straight from the container, then gradually reduce the amount you use.
- Try to add as little fat as possible when cooking vegetables such as onions. You can usually halve the amount called for in most recipes. (The amounts have been reduced in this book.)
- Try stir-frying using a steep-sided, round-bottomed pan like a wok. With it, you can cook food using only a small amount of oil.
- Invest in a nonstick pan and then you may not need to use any fat or oil at all. For example, when cooking ground beef, you can cook the beef without added fat. Pour off excess fat after cooking.
- Try microwaving, steaming, poaching, boiling or grilling instead of frying.

- Pot-roast or stew leaner cuts of meats, which are also less expensive. Remove all visible fat before cooking and drain fat during cooking. You don't need to brown the meat first.
- Make use of herbs and spices, onions, garlic, or lemon juice instead of butter to flavor foods, particularly vegetables.

Watch Out for Hidden Fats

You may think first of margarine and butter when you try to cut down on fat in your healthful eating plan. However, many foods, such as meat pies, cakes and cookies, contain large amounts of fat. These sources are often referred to as *hidden fat*. Some of these foods are listed on the next page. You may be surprised at the amount of fat they contain.

Cholesterol

Our bodies make cholesterol. It forms a necessary part of our cells and tissues. However, too much cholesterol in the blood causes a buildup of fatty deposits in the arteries, causing heart disease.

Some foods are naturally high in cholesterol. If you have high blood cholesterol levels, the general guideline is to limit the daily intake of cholesterol from your diet to 300 mg or less per day, but follow the advice of your physician. If you cut back the total amount of fat you ingest, particularly animal fat, you will automatically cut down on cholesterol. Bear in mind that it is the *total fat intake* and *types of fat* we eat that are important. It is best to cut down on foods high in saturated fats or to replace them with monounsaturated or polyunsaturated fats or oils.

Maintain a Healthful Weight

Being overweight makes the day-to-day control of your diabetes more difficult, so it is important to maintain a healthy weight. You will only lose weight if your body takes in fewer calories from food than you use up during the day as you go about your activities. Exercise should be part of your weight-loss plan, but you will still need to reduce the total amount of calories that you eat. The recipes in this book can help you. They are calorie-counted and lower in fat and sugar than standard recipes.

Hints for Losing Weight

- First, check with your physician to determine how much weight to lose.
- Decide that you really do want to lose weight. Be realistic when deciding how much you want to lose and set yourself short-term targets.
- Start slowly! Don't try to change your diet drastically overnight. Gradually try to improve your eating habits so you end up with a

Hidden Fats

Food	Average Fat Content
One large muffin	26 g
One large hamburger with cheese	24 g
One individual beef pot pie	24 g
One cup macaroni and cheese	22 g
One cup French vanilla ice cream	22 g
One order chicken nuggets	21 g
One piece quiche Lorraine	20 g
One-eighth coconut-cream pie	16 g
One glazed doughnut	16 g
One piece pepperoni pizza	12 g
One medium California avocado	12 g
One-eighth apple pie	12 g
One piece chocolate cake	11 g
One ounce potato chips	10 g
One piece cheese pizza	9 g
Two small chocolate-chip cookies	5 g

diet that will enable you to maintain a more healthful way of eating in the long term.

- Don't be tempted to jump on the scales every morning. Weigh yourself once a week, preferably on the same day and at the same time.
- Aim for a gradual but steady weight loss of 1 to 2 pounds per week. Anything more puts you in danger of losing essential lean tissue, such as muscle.
- Losing weight may take a long time, so it is important to reward yourself with a treat, such as a massage or movie tickets, when you reach your short-term goals (but do not reward yourself with food!).
- Include more exercise in your daily routine; for example, use the stairs instead of the elevator whenever possible.

Practical Tips

- Use the recipes and advice in this book to help you choose healthful, well-balanced, calorie-counted meals.
- Try to fill up on starchy carbohydrate foods and eat more fruit and vegetables. They have fewer calories and are more satisfying to eat, particularly the whole-grain varieties of starchy foods, including whole-grain bread, pasta or brown rice.
- Cut down on the amount of fat you eat. Fat is a concentrated form of calories. One gram of fat has more than twice as many calories as the same amount of protein or carbohydrate, so cutting down on fat intake is the quickest way to cut down on calories.
- Include some lower-fat dairy foods and lean meat and fish in your diet to make sure that you don't lose out on valuable minerals, vitamins and protein when losing weight.

Do Not Use Too Much Salt

Cutting down on salt can improve a high blood-pressure condition in some people.

Hints to Reduce Salt Intake

- Cut down on salty foods such as potato chips, salty snack foods and smoked meats and fish.
- Use fewer canned, packaged and processed foods, such as canned soups, which are often high in salt content.
- Try to avoid adding extra salt at the table and use less in cooking. Cut down gradually on the amount used so you have time to adjust to any change in taste. Most recipes in this book call for salt to taste and have been tested without any, or using only a minimum of salt.
- Use other flavorings in place of salt such as pepper, garlic, fresh herbs and spices.

Drink Alcohol Only in Moderation

If you have diabetes, there should be no reason why you cannot enjoy a drink with a meal, unless of course you have been advised to avoid alcohol for another medical reason. However, bear in mind that alcohol is high in calories, with little or no nutritional value; it does not contribute to a healthful eating plan. The recommended daily maximum alcohol intake for people with diabetes is the same as for everyone else: one or two drinks for men and one drink for women. It is also desirable to have two or three days a week without alcohol. One serving of alcohol equals 12 ounces of beer, 5 ounces of wine or 1.5 ounces of 80-proof distilled spirits.

If you are taking certain medicines or insulin for your diabetes, alcohol can contribute to *hypoglycemia* (low blood-glucose level). Drinking alcohol also makes it harder to recognize hypoglycemia and recover from it. It's important to bear in mind the following hints.

- Don't drink on an empty stomach or miss a meal so you can have a drink.

- If you drink beer, choose the ones with an alcohol content of less than 5 percent. Avoid malt liquors because they have a higher alcohol content.

- Use sugar-free mixers rather than the ordinary mixers.

- If you drink wine or sherry, choose the medium or dry varieties when you can, although the occasional sweet sherry is fine.

- Always wear some form of diabetes identification or carry a medical-alert card.

- Bear in mind that all types of alcoholic drinks are high in calories. If you are overweight or trying to lose weight, it is best to have only the occasional drink.

- You may be at risk of having hypoglycemia up to several hours after drinking alcohol. It is important therefore to have something to eat either before, with, or shortly after drinking alcohol. If you have had several drinks throughout the evening, be sure to have a substantial bedtime snack.

- Low-alcohol beers are useful, especially if you will be driving. However, it is best to check the amount of alcohol in each drink, because it is possible to go over the limit for driving even when drinking low-alcohol drinks all evening. It is always better to have a designated driver along if you plan to drink at all, or to be the designated driver yourself and not drink anything alcoholic.

AVOID DIABETIC FOOD PRODUCTS

Diabetic products are not recommended. There is no evidence that these foods and drinks offer an advantage to people with diabetes. They are expensive besides. They are not believed to be necessary as part of a healthful-eating plan.

FRUITS, VEGETABLES
AND THE VITAMIN CONNECTION

Recent studies have shown that eating more fruits and vegetables that are high in certain vitamins may actually reduce our risk of coronary heart disease. Vitamin C is one of the so-called antioxidant vitamins. The others are vitamins A (in the beta-carotene form) and E. Antioxidants are believed to have a neutralizing effect on cell-damaging, free-radical compounds in the body and therefore help keep us healthy. Large quantities of free radicals are created when the immune system goes into action to defend you against an infection. They are thought to contribute to the groggy feeling of a cold or the flu.

It is particularly important to have some foods rich in vitamin C every day. Vitamin C is water-soluble and cannot be stored in the body. This nutrient is used up faster during times of stress, which may explain why colds and infections seem to strike when we are feeling run-down or are not eating properly. Good natural sources of vitamin C are citrus fruits such as oranges, lemons and grapefruits, as well as rosehips, green bell peppers, parsley, potatoes and many other fresh fruits and vegetables.

Vitamin A, another antioxidant nutrient, is fat-soluble and can be stored in the body until needed, but it is still a good idea to keep reserves topped up. Good sources are liver and oily fish. It's not a good idea to take more than the recommended amount of vitamin A in supplements, such as tablets. Vitamin A can also be made in the body from beta carotene, which is plentiful in yellow- or orange-colored fruits and vegetables such as carrots, apricots, oranges, and dark-green vegetables such as spinach, greens and broccoli.

Vitamin E is found in tomatoes, sweet potatoes, chickpeas, wholegrain breads and cereals and certain oils, such as corn oil. Wheat germ also contains vitamin E. Store it in the refrigerator after opening, or it will turn rancid quickly.

The U.S. diet tends to be particularly low in fruits and vegetables, and the United States has one of the highest rates of heart disease internationally, so it is a good idea to eat more fruits and vegetables. In their Dietary Guidelines for Americans, the U.S. Departments of Agriculture and Health and Human Services recommend eating at least five servings of fruits and vegetables (excluding potatoes) each day. This may sound like a large amount, but remember that one serving is usually a 1/2 cup of cooked vegetables or one medium-size fruit.

PUTTING THE DAILY
RECOMMENDATIONS INTO PRACTICE

You may be wondering how all this advice relates to you and your day-to-day eating plan. The dietary recommendations for diabetes can be summarized very simply by the pie chart below.

A person who consumes about 2000 calories every day, for example, would need approximately 250 grams of carbohydrate, 80 grams of fat and 75 grams of protein per day. One gram of carbohydrates and protein have 4 calories and 1 gram of fat has 9 calories. Food labels show the calories and nutrient breakdown of canned and packaged foods, and they are helpful for comparison shopping.

The box on page 19 illustrates how you might achieve the right nutrient-and-calorie mix during one day.

Of course, you don't have to work out your daily menus this precisely. However, by following a healthful eating plan that is high in fiber and low in fat and sugar, you should find you are enjoying a balanced diet. Our example shows how easily you can achieve this goal.

Recommended Distribution of Energy Intake

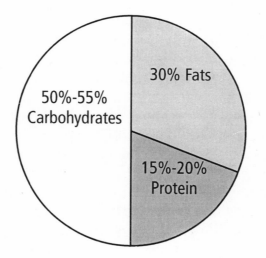

This chart shows that 50% to 55% of your daily calorie intake should come from starchy carbohydrate foods, 30% from fat in foods and 15% to 20% from protein.

Breakfast

2/3 cup bran flakes with 1/2 cup skim milk

1 slice whole-wheat toast with 1 teaspoon soft margarine

1 tablespoon all-fruit spread

Cup of tea/coffee with artificial sweetener

Mid-morning Snack

Medium banana

Cup of coffee/tea artificial sweetener

Lunch

Light Salad Niçoise (page 59)

2 slices whole-wheat or multi-grain bread

8 oz. no-sugar fruit yogurt

1 apple

No-calorie drink

Mid-afternoon Snack

1 orange

8 oz. skim milk

Evening Meal

Mushroom-and-Chicken Tagliatelle (page 107)

1/2 cup cooked green beans

Tossed green salad with 2 tablespoons fat-free dressing

1/2 cup fresh fruit salad

Evening Snack

1 slice Apricot-Pecan Slices (page 117) and 1/2 cup skim milk

or 1/2 sandwich with 1 oz. turkey breast

		Percentage of Caloric Intake
Calories	1765	
Fat	36 g	22%
Carbohydrate	278 g	60%
Protein	100 g	22%

EATING OUT

Having diabetes should not disrupt your lifestyle. You can certainly continue to enjoy the pleasures of dining out and eating away from home. If you only eat out on special occasions, don't feel guilty about eating something you would not normally eat, or overindulging a little. If you are watching your weight, try to avoid selections that are very high in fat and calories. But don't worry! There are usually other suitable, tempting dishes to choose from. If you eat out frequently (several times a week, for example), then you will probably need to think more carefully about the foods you choose. Try to avoid very rich or creamy sauces, too many fried foods or sweet desserts. Watch the amount of alcohol you have, too. You may find the following hints helpful when choosing from the menu.

- Choose main course dishes that are lower in fat and calories. Avoid fried dishes and those served with lots of butter or in rich sauces or dressings.
- Include generous portions of fresh vegetables or salad with your meal.
- Boiled or baked potatoes are a more healthful choice than French fries. If you do choose French fries, have a small portion.
- Keep in mind that most desserts at a restaurant are usually high in sugar and possibly fat. You may need to choose carefully, or eat a smaller portion.

Occasional indulgence in a meal when eating out may cause a temporary rise in blood sugar, but will not do long-term harm. **It is your day-to-day control that is important.** However, if you are concerned about eating out, you might want to ask your dietitian for some guidance. With experience and some trial and error, you will soon become more confident about which dishes to choose when dining away from home.

A SHOPPING GUIDE

Food shopping may seem a daunting prospect when you or a member of your family is newly diagnosed with diabetes. Don't despair! You'll do fine, especially if you spend a little extra time examining food labels more closely. If you find sugar first on the list of ingredients, then that product is *not* the best choice for everyday eating. However, if sugar is farther down the list (for example, "kidney beans, water, sugar, salt" listed on a can of kidney beans), the product is perfectly acceptable. Don't worry about the sugar content in canned vegetables, soups, high-fiber cereals, and so on, because the scant amount present in these foods should not affect your diabetes control.

You do not need to follow a totally sugar-free diet. It's really only pure sugar, candies and very sugary foods that you need to replace or eat in moderation. Many reduced-sugar or sugar-free products now available in supermarkets are suitable. These include sugar-free gelatin desserts, sugar-free dessert toppings, diet yogurts and canned fruit in natural juice. Other desserts can be made at home based on fresh fruit, such as a fresh-fruit salad.

You may be concerned about ice cream, but you don't need to avoid this altogether. The more expensive premium brands contain more fat and calories, so the standard brands are usually a better choice. Look for the reduced-fat and reduced-sugar versions that are available, too.

Sugar-sweetened drinks are best avoided except when treating hypoglycemia. You can substitute with sugar-free or diet drinks instead. For information on artificial sweeteners, please see pages 9-11.

Breakfast Cereals

The wide range of breakfast cereals available can be confusing to choose from. Many varieties are coated with sugar. However, more healthful varieties can be found, if you're choosy. Read the labels and check for amounts of sugar and fiber. If you usually sprinkle sugar over your breakfast cereal, then you could use a granulated artificial sweetener instead. Sweeteners are usually located near the sugar in supermarkets.

Breads and Spreads

You'll find a vast array of breads to choose from. Whole-grain bread is widely available. If you or your family won't eat whole-grain bread, buy high-fiber white bread. If you usually have jam or marmalade on your bread or toast, you may be pleased to know that most supermarkets stock reduced-sugar jams and marmalades.

Dairy Products

Dairy products such as milk, cheese and cream are usually high in fat, but there are many lowfat, reduced-fat and nonfat alternatives. These include skim or lowfat milk, reduced-fat cheeses and reduced-fat margarines or lowfat spreads.

Oils and Fats

Polyunsaturated oils, such as soybean, corn, safflower or sunflower, are good choices. Olive oil and canola oil are high in monounsaturated fats. Try to include some of both kinds of fats in your diet. The type of fat to avoid is the kind that is saturated. (Saturated fats become hard at room temperature.) Saturated fats include butter, solid vegetable shortening, hard margarines and the fats from coconut oil and palm oil, as well as some of the fat in meats and dairy products.

Pasta and Rice

Pasta is good to include in the weekly shopping basket. Whole-wheat pasta is higher in fiber, but any type of pasta is suitable for healthful eating, providing it is not smothered in high-fat sauces. Brown or white rice is also a good choice.

Fruits and Vegetables

In their Dietary Guidelines for Americans, the U.S. Departments of Agriculture and Health and Human Services recommend eating at least five servings of fruits and vegetables each day, excluding potatoes (considered a bread-group food for people with diabetes).

Fruit and vegetables are important to include in your diet. They contain valuable vitamins, minerals and fiber. Many people with diabetes are concerned about eating fruit because of the natural sugar it contains. Perhaps you were told not to eat too many grapes and to eat only small bananas. Grapes are very sweet; you could easily eat a whole bunch. This isn't advisable, because in doing so you would consume a lot of carbohydrates at once. A large banana may contain carbohydrates equivalent to two or three pieces of fruit, which may also be too much to eat at one time. However, most everyday fruits—such as apples, pears and oranges—are naturally portioned in reasonable amounts. It is a good idea to include fruit after a meal or as a snack.

Legumes

Lentils and beans are an excellent addition to healthful eating because they are a good source of soluble fiber. They may be purchased dried. Many are available in cans, including kidney beans, chickpeas and lentils.

Meat, Poultry and Fish

Two or three servings of food in this category can be included as part of a healthful daily eating plan. Look for lean cuts of meat and remove all visible fat before cooking. Some supermarkets sell meat that is already trimmed of fat. Extra-lean ground beef is now widely available. Ground turkey and chicken may be high in fat. Eat fish occasionally.

Desserts and Sweets

Plain cookies are suitable to include as snacks; so are cereal bars. You'll find that some cookies are available in a lower-fat or "light" version, but check the label; the difference in fat and calories may not be significant. You may eat a small amount of sweets or dessert at the end of a high-fiber meal or on special occasions, as long as they are calculated to fit in as part your overall daily carbohydrate count.

Additional Help

Many supermarkets produce information leaflets about healthful eating that are displayed prominently in the store. Processed foods indicate on the nutritional label whether the product is high-fiber, lowfat and so forth. Nutritional labeling is extremely useful if you are trying to choose wisely from among foods that seem similar.

ABOUT THE RECIPES

All the recipes in this cookbook have been developed according to the very latest dietary guidelines. Where possible, the recipes are high in fiber, low (or lower than usual) in fat and low in sugar.

Each recipe has been carefully tried and tested using the most healthful ingredients—all easily available from supermarkets. Good nutrition, taste, variety and enjoyment of food have certainly not been forgotten! I consider them absolutely essential to a healthful-eating plan. I hope you will agree that there are recipes to suit various occasions and palates, with an emphasis on the Mediterranean style of eating. Some are classics you will recognize, but I have adapted them to suit a healthful lifestyle.

Adapting Your Own Recipes

Many people feel that they will be unable to use favorite recipes or cookbooks once they have been diagnosed with diabetes. Following a healthful eating plan does not mean mastering a whole new repertoire of recipes. You can modify your own recipes by reducing the amount of saturated fat and sugar they contain and increasing the fiber.

Try the recipes in this book to give you some ideas. With a little practice, you will soon find it easy to adapt your own family favorites to be high in fiber, low in fat and low in sugar—without compromising taste. The following hints should help.

- If a recipe uses ordinary white flour, try substituting part whole-wheat flour to increase the fiber content. You may need to add a little more liquid when using whole-wheat flour to keep the mixture as moist as it should be.
- Use a lowfat vegetable-oil spread or soft tub margarine in place of butter or hard margarine to reduce the fat and calories. Lowfat vegetable-oil spreads are not suitable for all baked recipes, but soft margarines are a useful alternative in those cases. Use polyunsaturated margarines, which have the advantage of containing a fat that is somewhat better for your heart.
- You can reduce the sugar content of most cake recipes by one-third to one-half. As you and your family get used to a less-sweet taste, you may find that for some recipes, particularly fruitcakes or quick breads, you don't need to add any sugar, but can rely on the dried fruit for sweetness.

- Using lowfat or nonfat milk for cooking reduces the fat content of a dish. (Remember that nonfat milk is not recommended for children under two years of age.)

- When making puddings, omit the sugar and use artificial sweetener instead. Add the sweetener once the pudding has thickened and cooled slightly. Other sweet sauces can be made in a similar way. Replace the milk with skim or lowfat milk to reduce the fat and calories.

- For recipes using ground beef, cook without adding extra oil when browning the beef, particularly if you are using a nonstick pan. Choose lean or extra-lean beef where possible. Drain off excess fat after browning.

- If oil is called for in a recipe, try to reduce the amount. Remember that 1 tablespoon of oil has about 100 calories!

- Choose oils that are high in monounsaturated fat, such as olive or canola oil, or polyunsaturated fat, such as corn or sunflower oil.

- Reduce the amount of meat called for in recipes. Instead, include more vegetables (such as carrots) or legumes (such as lentils). This helps increase the fiber in the dish, increases the number of servings and is less expensive. A good example is to add a small can of beans or lentils to a spaghetti sauce or casserole. (Remember that you are adding extra carbohydrate to the total recipe when you do so.)

Carbohydrate Content of the Recipes

If you have insulin-dependent diabetes, you may have been advised to keep to a daily carbohydrate allowance or a certain number of food exchanges. All of the recipes in this book have been calculated to give the total carbohydrate (as well as protein, fat and calories) per serving and food exchanges so that you can see at a glance how to fit them into your food plan.

NUTRITIONAL ANALYSIS

Nutritional analysis was calculated using *The Food Processor® for Windows* software program, version 6.0, copyright 1987-1995 by ESHA Research. It has a database of more than 10,000 foods and provides analysis for 113 nutrients and 21 nutrient factors, including food exchanges. It uses data from the USDA and other scientific sources.

Analysis given in this book does not include optional ingredients or variations. Where an ingredient amount is a range, the higher number is used. Where there is a range of servings, the lower number is used.

Starters

I've included a range of starters, from fat-free dishes, such as a fruit-filled melon, to filling soups. The soups, such as Leek and Cheese or Italian Red Bean and Pasta, could also be used as a light lunch served with fresh crusty bread.

Black-eyed Pea and Vegetable Soup

Black-eyed peas are an attractive addition with their creamy color and small black "eye." They add a creamy flavor, too. Remember to soak the dried beans before starting this recipe.

If you don't have time to soak beans or legumes overnight, you can use the quick-soak method. Cover them with boiling rather than cold water and soak only 2 to 3 hours, or bring them slowly to a boil in a large pan of water. Simmer 5 minutes, cover, turn off the heat and soak only 1 hour.

6	oz. dried black-eyed peas
1	tablespoon olive or sunflower oil
2	medium onions, finely diced
1	garlic clove, crushed
2	carrots, peeled and finely diced
1	green bell pepper, finely diced
2	large zucchini, sliced
6	cups vegetable stock
	Salt and freshly ground black pepper
	Freshly chopped parsley to garnish

Soak the peas overnight in enough cold water to cover. Drain. Heat the oil in a large saucepan over medium heat. Add the onion and cook until soft. Add the garlic, carrots, bell pepper and zucchini and cook 2 minutes. Add the stock and drained beans. Boil 10 minutes. Reduce heat, cover and simmer 50 minutes until the beans are tender. Season with salt and pepper and serve sprinkled with chopped parsley.

Makes 4 to 6 servings.

Each serving contains:

				Exchanges:	
Calories	259	Total Fat	4g	Bread	1.9
Protein	13g	Saturated Fat	1g	Vegetable	2.3
Carbohydrates	45g	Cholesterol	0mg	Meat	0.1
Fiber	9g	Sodium	174mg		

Leek and Cheese Soup

The inspiration for this recipe came from a delicious soup served at a friend's wedding reception. I decided to experiment at home to develop a similar recipe. I think the flavors of leek and blue cheese complement each other well.

Leeks are difficult to clean if you want to keep them whole. For a recipe like this, where they are to be puréed, slice the leeks lengthwise first and then across. The layers will separate and you can rinse them thoroughly in a colander under running water.

1	tablespoon olive or corn oil
1	large onion, chopped
1-1/2	lb. leeks, sliced
1	tablespoon all-purpose flour
3	cups vegetable or chicken stock
3	tablespoons dry white wine
	Salt and freshly ground black pepper
2	oz. blue cheese, crumbled
1/2	cup 2% lowfat milk

Heat the oil in a heavy saucepan over medium heat. Add the onion and leeks and cook 5 minutes or until softened, but not colored. Stir in the flour and cook 1 minute. Remove the pan from the heat and gradually stir in the stock, wine, salt and pepper. Return the pan to the heat and bring to a boil, stirring constantly. Reduce the heat and simmer, uncovered, 20 to 30 minutes or until onion is tender.

Process in a food processor or blender until smooth. Return to the rinsed-out pan and add the cheese and milk. Heat over low heat, stirring constantly, until cheese melts. Season to taste. Serve hot with a whole-wheat roll.

Makes 4 to 6 servings.

Each serving contains:				*Exchanges*:	
Calories	248	Total Fat	9g	Bread	0.2
Protein	8g	Saturated Fat	4g	Vegetable	5.8
Carbohydrates	36g	Cholesterol	13mg	Meat	0.4
Fiber	6g	Sodium	392mg	Fat	1.5

Quick Chickpea Dip

On returning from a vacation in Crete, we held a 'Greek night' for friends and I made this dish. It is simple to make and will impress your guests, who will believe you bought it! Tahini is a sesame paste, available in delicatessens and many supermarkets. Use small lemons—otherwise they may overpower the flavor of the dip.

1	(14-oz.) can chickpeas, drained
	Juice of 2 small lemons
1/4	cup tahini paste
3	garlic cloves, crushed
	Pinch cayenne pepper
1	tablespoon chopped fresh parsley to garnish

Place the chickpeas in a food processor or blender with the lemon juice. Blend until smooth. Add the tahini, garlic and cayenne pepper and process until blended. Spoon into a serving bowl. Sprinkle with parsley and chill before serving. Serve with warm pita bread.

Makes 4 to 6 servings.

Each serving contains:

Calories	183	Total Fat	10g	Fat	2.0
Protein	7g	Saturated Fat	1g		
Carbohydrates	18g	Cholesterol	0mg		
Fiber	7g	Sodium	214mg		

Exchanges:

Italian Red Bean and Pasta Soup

A filling, lowfat dish, this soup is also suitable for a lunch or light supper. You can use any pasta, but look for small varieties, made especially for soup. They come in a variety of shapes, some of which are particularly appealing to children.

2	teaspoons olive or sunflower oil
1	medium onion, finely diced
4	stalks celery, sliced
1/2	teaspoon dried thyme
1	(7-oz.) can red kidney beans, rinsed and drained
1	(14-oz.) can chopped tomatoes
2-1/2	cups vegetable stock
	Salt and freshly ground black pepper
2	oz. whole-wheat small macaroni or other pasta

Heat the oil in a large saucepan over medium heat. Add the onion, celery and thyme and cook 4 to 5 minutes, stirring occasionally. Add the beans, tomatoes, stock, salt and pepper. Bring to a boil. Reduce heat, cover and simmer 30 minutes. Add the pasta and cook 10 to 12 minutes or until the pasta is tender. Serve hot with fresh whole-wheat bread.

Makes 2 to 3 servings.

Kidney beans make a colorful addition to a soup. Canned ones are easy and quick to use but if you decide to use dried kidney beans, boil them 10 to 15 minutes before reducing the heat and simmering until tender.

Each serving contains:

Calories	441	Total Fat	15g	Bread	2.7
Protein	16g	Saturated Fat	2g	Vegetable	4.1
Carbohydrates	66g	Cholesterol	0mg	Fat	2.6
Fiber	16g	Sodium	680mg		

Exchanges:

Quick Tomato Salsa

This dish is as colorful as the Latino big-band dance music with which it shares its name. You can vary the amount of hot pepper sauce according to how spicy you like your food. Salsa is a popular Mexican dish usually served with tortilla chips.

This dip is delicious with potato skins.

1	(14-oz.) can chopped tomatoes, drained
1	small onion, very finely chopped
1	(4-oz.) can green chiles, drained
2	garlic cloves, crushed
1	tablespoon white-wine vinegar
1	tablespoon tomato paste
1	tablespoon lemon juice
1/2	teaspoon hot pepper sauce
	Freshly ground black pepper

Combine all the ingredients together in a small bowl. Cover and chill until required. Serve with tortilla chips.

Makes 6 servings.

Each serving contains:

				Exchanges:
Calories	26	Total Fat	0g	Vegetable 1.0
Protein	1g	Saturated Fat	0g	
Carbohydrates	6g	Cholesterol	0mg	
Fiber	1g	Sodium	351mg	

Chilled Summer Gazpacho

A refreshing chilled soup to serve in the summer with fresh crusty bread. Depending on the capacity of your food processor or blender, you may find it easier to process the vegetables in stages before adding the remaining ingredients to get a smoother result. Chill the soup thoroughly before serving.

2	lb. ripe tomatoes, roughly chopped
1	large onion, roughly chopped
1	green bell pepper, seeded and chopped
1	medium cucumber, chopped
3	tablespoons red-wine vinegar
1	tablespoon olive oil
2	garlic cloves, crushed
2-1/2	cups canned crushed tomatoes in purée
	Salt and freshly ground black pepper

Place the fresh tomatoes in a food processor or blender and blend a few seconds. Add the onion, bell pepper and cucumber and process until smooth. Add the remaining ingredients and process a few more seconds. Place in a large serving bowl, cover and chill before serving.

Makes 6 to 8 servings.

Serve this colorful soup with a vegetable garnish. Chop some extra or reserve a little of the tomato, bell pepper, onion and cucumber for sprinkling on top of the soup before serving. It is also delicious served with garlic croutons.

Lowfat Garlic Croutons

Cream a little soft margarine with a crushed garlic clove. Spread on a thick slice of bread. Cut into cubes and put on a baking sheet. Bake at 400F (205C) 10 minutes or until crisp and golden.

Each serving contains:

				Exchanges:	
Calories	116	Total Fat	3g	Vegetable	3.6
Protein	4g	Saturated Fat	0g		
Carbohydrates	23g	Cholesterol	0mg		
Fiber	5g	Sodium	520mg		

Spicy Chicken Satay with Peanut Dip

Patio Picnic

These tasty satay appetizers could also be served as a summer main course for a patio lunch or a picnic. Serve with fresh crusty bread, pasta salad and a green salad. This quantity serves 4.

Note: Soak the wooden cocktail picks in hot water for 3 minutes before using them so they will not char in the oven.

Delicious to nibble! Don't worry if the dip looks lightly curdled after cooking. Simply cool it completely, then beat in the milk. Give the dip a quick stir before serving.

1	lb. skinless, boneless chicken breasts
1	small onion, finely chopped
1	garlic clove, crushed
2	tablespoons low-sodium soy sauce
2	tablespoons white-wine vinegar
1	teaspoon olive or sunflower oil
1	teaspoon mild curry powder
1	teaspoon chili powder
1/2	cup natural peanut butter
1	cup water
1	tablespoon nonfat milk
1/2	small cucumber

Place the chicken between two sheets of waxed paper and flatten with a rolling pin. Cut into 1-inch pieces and place in a shallow container. Mix the onion and garlic with the soy sauce and vinegar. Pour over the chicken and toss well. Cover and refrigerate overnight.

Meanwhile, make the dip. Heat the oil in a small pan. Add the curry and chili powder and cook 30 to 60 seconds, stirring. Add the peanut butter and water. Simmer 2 to 3 minutes, stirring constantly, or until thickened. Allow to cool completely, then stir in the milk. Refrigerate until required.

Preheat oven to 425F (220C). Thread the chicken on plain wooden cocktail picks and place on a baking sheet. Bake 10 to 15 minutes or until cooked through, turning halfway through cooking. Brush with the marinade during the first 5 minutes of cooking only. Chill until required. Just before serving, cut the cucumber into 1/2-inch pieces and thread onto the picks with the chicken. Serve the chicken and cucumber cold with the peanut dip.

Makes about 40.

Each chicken piece contains:

Calories	14	Total Fat	0g	
Protein	2g	Saturated Fat	0g	
Carbohydrates	0g	Cholesterol	6mg	
Fiber	0g	Sodium	71mg	

Exchanges:
Meat 0.2

Each tablespoon dip contains:

Calories	30	Total Fat	3g	
Protein	1g	Saturated Fat	0g	
Carbohydrates	1g	Cholesterol	0mg	
Fiber	0g	Sodium	13mg	

Exchanges:
none

Spicy Winter Mulligatawny

Mulligatawny first became popular in Britain at the end of the eighteenth century when it was brought back by employees of the East India Company who had been stationed overseas. It was changed for British cooks and is traditionally seasoned with curry powder quite different from the spice blends that would have been used in the South-Indian original. The word comes from the Tamil words for "pepper" and "water."

For a vegetarian dish, omit the chicken and use a good vegetable stock. It won't spoil the flavor. Serve with fresh whole-wheat bread.

2	tablespoons soft margarine
1	large onion, finely chopped
2	garlic cloves, crushed
2	stalks celery, sliced
2	carrots, peeled and diced
1 to 2	tablespoons curry powder
1	tablespoon all-purpose flour
1	tablespoon tomato paste
4	cups chicken stock
1	medium apple, peeled, cored and diced
4	oz. cooked lean chicken, diced

Melt the margarine in a large saucepan over medium heat. Add the onion, garlic, celery and carrots and cook, stirring occasionally, 3 to 4 minutes or until soft. Stir in the curry powder and flour and cook, stirring, 1 minute. Stir in the tomato paste and gradually add the stock. Add the apple and bring to a boil. Reduce heat, cover and simmer 20 minutes.

Remove from the heat. Process in a food processor a few seconds to finely chop. Return to the saucepan, add the diced chicken and heat until the chicken is heated through. Serve hot.

Makes 4 to 6 servings.

Each serving contains:

Calories	182	Total Fat	8g	Bread	0.1
Protein	12g	Saturated Fat	2g	Vegetable	1.2
Carbohydrates	16g	Cholesterol	16mg	Meat	0.5
Fiber	3g	Sodium	905mg		

Exchanges:

Hearty Winter Vegetable Soup

Pearl barley is an excellent addition to vegetable soups. It has an interesting texture and flavor but more important, the protein it contains combines with the other vegetable proteins to make a complete protein. The body can use this type more efficiently than protein from the vegetables and grains if they are served separately.

A nourishing soup that makes use of fresh vegetables in season. It is ideal as a low-calorie lunch, served with whole-wheat bread.

1	tablespoon olive or sunflower oil
1	large onion, finely chopped
1	medium rutabaga, cubed
2	large carrots, diced
1	medium turnip, diced
2	leeks, sliced
1/2	cup pearl barley
1	teaspoon mixed dried herbs
4	cups vegetable stock
	Salt and freshly ground black pepper
2	tablespoons chopped fresh parsley

Heat the oil in a large saucepan over medium heat. Add the vegetables, cover and cook 5 minutes or until soft. Add the barley and cook, stirring occasionally, 2 to 3 minutes.

Stir in the herbs, stock, salt and pepper. Bring to a boil. Reduce heat, cover and simmer 45 minutes or until the vegetables are tender. Adjust seasoning and serve sprinkled with parsley. Serve with whole-wheat bread.

Makes 4 servings.

Each serving contains:

				Exchanges:	
Calories	231	Total Fat	4g	Bread	1.1
Protein	5g	Saturated Fat	1g	Vegetable	4.0
Carbohydrates	46g	Cholesterol	0mg	Fat	0.7
Fiber	10g	Sodium	199mg		

Cheese-and-Spinach Filo Triangles

Little nibbles like these that are easy to pick up are great for starters at a bar-becue party. They can be made well in advance and popped in the oven at the last minute. They don't compete for space on the grill, and with such tasty morsels, guests won't mind waiting while the main course cooks.

These triangles look impressive, yet are fairly simple to make. They resemble East Indian samosas, but because they are baked rather than fried, they are lower in fat and calories.

1	(1-lb.) pkg. frozen chopped spinach, thawed
1	(8-oz.) container fat-free cream cheese
1	garlic clove, crushed
1/4	teaspoon grated nutmeg
	Grated peel of half a lemon
	Salt and freshly ground black pepper
6	sheets filo pastry, thawed, if frozen
1/4	cup polyunsaturated margarine, melted

Preheat oven to 400F (205C). Lightly grease a large baking sheet. Cook the spinach in a saucepan over medium heat about 10 minutes, stirring occasionally. Press in a sieve to drain any remaining water and set aside to cool. Place the cheese, garlic, nutmeg and lemon peel in a bowl. Beat in the spinach, salt and pepper and mix thoroughly. Keep the filo pastry under a damp towel while working. Brush one pastry sheet at a time with a little melted margarine and cut each sheet lengthwise into 3 pieces.

Barbecue Party

Cheese-and-Spinach Filo Triangles

Marinated Chicken and Rosemary Kebabs (page 98)

Tomato and Red Onion Salad (page 58)

Garlic Bread

Apricot Upside-Down Cake (page 132)

Place a heaping teaspoonful of cheese mixture at one end. Fold the pastry over diagonally and keep folding until you reach the end. Continue until all the pastry sheets and filling have been used. Place the triangles on a greased baking sheet and brush the tops with the remaining margarine. Bake 8 to 10 minutes or until golden brown. Serve hot.

Makes about 24.

Each triangle contains:				*Exchanges:*	
Calories	43	Total Fat	2g	Bread	0.2
Protein	2g	Saturated Fat	0g	Vegetable	0.1
Carbohydrates	4g	Cholesterol	1mg	Fat	0.4
Fiber	0g	Sodium	118mg		

Fruit-filled Melon

These attractive fruit-filled melon halves make a light, refreshing start to a special meal and are a good way of introducing some extra fruit into your diet.

A ripe melon will yield a little at the flower end (opposite end of the stalk), but the best way to tell if a melon of this type is ripe is to smell it. Sniff for a sweet, heady, musky perfume from a ripe fruit.

3   small cantaloupe or other small melons
2   medium grapefruits
1   orange
5   oz. frozen raspberries, defrosted and drained
      Grated peel and juice of 1 lime
      A little artificial sweetener (optional)
      Sprigs of fresh mint to garnish

Cut the melons in half and discard the seeds. Scoop out a little of the flesh from the center of each half with a melon baller and place in a bowl. Peel and segment the grapefruits and orange, saving the juice. Cut the segments in half and place in the bowl, together with the juice and raspberries. Divide the fruit among the melon halves. Sprinkle with a little lime juice, the grated peel and sweetener, if using. Refrigerate and serve chilled. Finish each half with a mint sprig.

Makes 6 servings.

Each serving contains:

Calories	140	Total Fat	1g	Fruit	2.6
Protein	3g	Saturated Fat	0g		
Carbohydrates	34g	Cholesterol	0mg		
Fiber	5g	Sodium	24mg		

Exchanges:
Fruit   2.6

Fish

We should all eat fish more frequently. Fish could almost be referred to as *fast food*, because it cooks in just minutes. You can purchase fish, fresh or frozen, ready to cook. The lighter in color, the milder the flavor and the less fat the fish contains. Its mild flavor is enlivened with ginger, cilantro, red pepper and a variety of herbs. Oily fish, such as mackerel, sardines and herring, are particularly valuable in the diet. They contain omega-3 fatty acids, which appear to have a unique way of protecting against heart disease. Oily fish is also particularly rich in vitamins A and D.

Fish with Ginger and Cilantro

Fresh ginger is becoming increasingly popular. It is available from the produce section in supermarkets. It keeps well in the refrigerator several days. Store in a plastic bag to prevent drying out.

A delicious and unusual way of serving fish. Serve with noodles and finely shredded vegetables.

4	trout, cleaned and filleted
1	leek, trimmed and finely sliced
1	medium carrot, trimmed and cut into very fine sticks
1	zucchini, trimmed and cut into matchstick pieces
1	(1-inch) piece fresh ginger, peeled and grated
1/4	cup chopped fresh cilantro
	Salt and freshly ground black pepper
2	tablespoons low-sodium soy sauce
1	garlic clove, crushed
1/4	cup dry white wine

Preheat oven to 400F (205C). Cut 4 rectangles of parchment paper or foil large enough to wrap around each fish. Place a fish in the center of each rectangle. Arrange the leek, carrot, zucchini, ginger and cilantro on top of each fish. Season with salt and pepper.

Mix together the soy sauce, garlic and wine in a small bowl and spoon over the fish. Fold in the edges to seal each package tightly. Place packages on a large baking sheet.

Bake 30 minutes or until the fish flakes when pierced with a fork.

Makes 4 servings.

Each serving contains:

Calories	292	Total Fat	9g	
Protein	42g	Saturated Fat	2g	
Carbohydrates	8g	Cholesterol	197mg	
Fiber	1g	Sodium	537mg	

Exchanges:

Vegetable	1.2
Meat	6.5
Fat	0.2

Flaky Salmon-and-Asparagus Tart

A colorful, savory tart that is particularly suitable for a luncheon or buffet. Make this for a late-spring treat served on the patio.

Spring High Tea for Six

Flaky Salmon-and-
Asparagus Tart
*(opposite) served with
Creamy Curried Potato
Salad (page 66) and
Tomato and Red Onion
Salad (page 58) with
fresh crusty bread;*

Apricot Pecan Slice
(page 117)

1/2	cup all-purpose flour
1/2	cup whole-wheat flour
1/4	cup soft margarine
6	asparagus spears
1	(7-oz.) can salmon, drained, flaked and bones removed
2	eggs
1/2	cup nonfat milk
	Salt and freshly ground black pepper

Sift the flours into a bowl. Add any bran remaining in the sifter back into the bowl. Cut in the margarine until the mixture resembles fine bread crumbs. Add enough cold water to mix to a soft dough. Shape into a ball, cover and refrigerate 30 minutes.

Preheat oven to 400F (205C). Roll out dough on a lightly floured board to a 10-inch circle. Use to line an 8-inch tart pan. Blanch the asparagus in boiling salted water 5 minutes. Cool in iced water. Arrange salmon in bottom of pastry shell. Drain asparagus and arrange on top of the salmon. Beat the eggs, milk, salt and pepper together in a small bowl. Pour over asparagus.

Bake 35 to 40 minutes or until filling is set. Serve either hot or cold.

Makes 6 servings.

Each serving contains:

				Exchanges:	
				Bread	0.9
Calories	225	Total Fat	12g	Vegetable	0.1
Protein	12g	Saturated Fat	2g	Milk	0.1
Carbohydrates	17g	Cholesterol	86mg	Meat	1.2
Fiber	2g	Sodium	369mg	Fat	1.7

Red Pepper, Basil and Tuna Pasta Salad

Choose tuna packed in water rather than oil to reduce the fat content and calories. If you drain oil-packed tuna, you drain away 15% to 25% of the health-giving omega-3 fatty acids that leach from the fish into the oil. Draining waterpacked tuna loses only about 3% of these beneficial fatty acids.

I often make a pasta salad for my husband to take to work as a change from sandwiches, or for the family as a weekend lunch. Serve with a mixed vegetable or green salad.

2	(7-oz.) cans tuna packed in water, drained
10	oz. whole-wheat pasta twists, cooked
4	oz. green beans, trimmed and sliced
1	red bell pepper, seeded and diced
2	tablespoons chopped fresh basil
1-1/2	oz. ripe olives, halved
1/4	cup olive oil
1/2	teaspoon whole-grain mustard
2	tablespoons white-wine vinegar
1	garlic clove (optional), crushed

Flake the tuna and place in a large serving bowl; add pasta.

Cook the green beans and bell pepper in lightly salted boiling water 2 to 3 minutes or until crisp-tender. Drain and refresh in cold water. Add to the tuna with the pasta, basil and olives. Cover and refrigerate 1 hour. Shake the remaining ingredients in a jar with a tight-fitting lid to make a dressing. Add dressing to the salad in the bowl, toss to combine and serve.

Makes 4 to 6 servings.

Each serving contains:

				Exchanges:	
Calories	520	Total Fat	18g	Bread	2.9
Protein	38g	Saturated Fat	3g	Vegetable	0.6
Carbohydrates	55g	Cholesterol	42mg	Meat	4.0
Fiber	9g	Sodium	486mg	Fat	2.9

Tiger Prawn Jambalaya

I find fresh tiger prawns are rather expensive for a weekday meal, but this makes a great informal supper dish for friends. Serve with a green salad.

2	tablespoons olive or sunflower oil
2	large onions, finely diced
2	red bell peppers, seeded and finely diced
6	stalks celery, thinly sliced
1	cup fish stock or chicken broth
1	cup canned crushed plum tomatoes in purée
1	teaspoon cayenne pepper
1	tablespoon chopped fresh thyme
2	bay leaves
	Salt and freshly ground black pepper
1	cup brown rice
1	lb. fresh raw tiger prawns
	Chopped fresh parsley and lemon wedges to garnish

Heat the oil in a nonstick skillet over medium-low heat. Add the onions, bell peppers and celery. Cook 5 to 10 minutes, stirring occasionally, until softened. Stir in the stock, tomatoes, cayenne pepper, thyme, bay leaves, salt and pepper. Bring to a boil, cover and simmer 30 minutes.

Meanwhile, cook the rice according to the package instructions. Drain and keep warm.

Peel the prawns, leaving on the tails. Add the prawns to the sauce mixture and cook 3 to 5 minutes or until the prawns turn pink. Serve with the rice, garnished with parsley and lemon wedges.

Makes 4 servings.

Tiger prawns are very attractive with their distinctive stripes. If you buy them frozen, check if they are in a protective ice glaze, and if this is included in the weight. Sometimes the ice accounts for almost half of the package weight.

Each serving contains:

Calories	412	Total Fat	10g	Bread	2.0
Protein	30g	Saturated Fat	1g	Vegetable	2.5
Carbohydrates	51g	Cholesterol	0mg	Meat	2.5
Fiber	5g	Sodium	483mg		

Exchanges:

Baked Fresh Salmon and Spinach in Light Pastry

4th of July Dinner

For a dinner party for eight:
Chilled Fruit-filled Melon (page 38)—use 4 melons and 8 oz. raspberries for 8 people

Baked Fresh Salmon and Spinach in Light Pastry (opposite), served with new potatoes, baby carrots and snow peas

Light Cheesecake (page 153)

This recipe takes a little time to prepare but is worth the effort. It is especially impressive to serve when entertaining. Serve with boiled new potatoes and fresh vegetables.

	Grated peel and juice of 1/2 lemon
	Salt and freshly ground black pepper
1	tablespoon chopped fresh dill
2	fresh salmon fillets, about 10 oz. each
1	(17-oz.) pkg. puff pastry, thawed if frozen
1	(10-oz.) pkg. frozen chopped spinach, thawed and squeezed dry
4	oz. fat-free cream cheese
4	oz. brown mushrooms, sliced
1	egg, beaten

Combine the lemon juice and peel, black pepper and dill in a small bowl. Rub the mixture into the salmon, and place in a nonmetallic dish. Cover and marinate in the refrigerator at least 1 hour.

Preheat oven to 400F (205C). Keep half the pastry chilled. Roll out remaining half of the pastry on a lightly floured surface to a rectangle measuring about 14 x 6 inches. Place on a large baking sheet and prick all over with a fork. Bake 12 to 15 minutes or until golden brown and cooked through. Cool on a wire rack.

Meanwhile, mix the spinach and cream cheese together and season to taste with salt and pepper. Return the cooked pastry to the baking sheet and arrange the salmon fillets on top, skinned side down. Spread the spinach mixture over the salmon, then layer with the sliced mushrooms.

Roll out the remaining pastry to approximately 15 x 8 inches and place over the salmon and vegetables to completely cover. Trim off any excess pastry. Slash the pastry to form a lattice pattern. Glaze all over with beaten egg. Bake 30 to 40 minutes or until the fish flakes when pierced with a fork and the pastry is puffed and golden brown. Serve hot.

Makes 8 to 10 servings.

Each serving contains:				*Exchanges:*	
Calories	498	Total Fat	29g	Bread	1.8
Protein	28g	Saturated Fat	5g	Vegetable	0.5
Carbohydrates	31g	Cholesterol	68mg	Meat	2.6
Fiber	2g	Sodium	362mg	Fat	4.3

Zesty Lemon Fish in Packages

A quick, attractive way to serve white fish. Serve with steamed rice and freshly cooked vegetables.

1	medium zucchini, cut into thin strips
1	lemon, thinly sliced
1	large carrot, peeled and cut into very thin strips
4	oz. button mushrooms, sliced
4	(6-oz.) fish fillets, such as snapper or other white fish
1/4	cup dry white wine
	Freshly ground black pepper

Preheat oven to 400F (205C). Cut 4 rectangles of parchment paper or foil large enough to wrap around each fish fillet. Divide half the zucchini, lemon, carrot and mushrooms among the rectangles. Lay a fish fillet on top of each portion and scatter the remaining vegetables and lemon over the top. Sprinkle with the wine and season with salt and pepper. Fold in the edges to seal each package tightly. Place packages on baking sheets. Bake 10 to 15 minutes. Serve at the table in the packages for everyone to open.

Makes 4 servings.

Tip

Use a vegetable peeler to make very thin strips of carrot and zucchini.

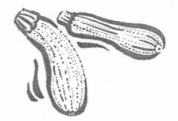

Each serving contains:

				Exchanges:	
Calories	244	Total Fat	3g	Vegetable	0.6
Protein	46g	Saturated Fat	1g	Meat	4.8
Carbohydrates	3g	Cholesterol	80mg	Fat	0.2
Fiber	1g	Sodium	105mg		

Baked Fish with Citrus and Cilantro Stuffing

Almost any fish fillets can be used in this recipe. Orange or grapefruit can be substituted for the lemons.

1	tablespoon olive or sunflower oil
1	medium onion, finely chopped
1/2	cup fresh whole-wheat bread crumbs
3	tablespoons chopped fresh cilantro
1	egg, beaten
	Salt and freshly ground black pepper
4	fresh trout, cleaned and boned
	Grated peel and juice of 2 lemons

Preheat oven to 375F (190C). Lightly grease a baking dish. Heat the oil in a small saucepan over medium heat. Add the onion and cook 2 to 3 minutes or until soft. Drain on paper towels. Transfer the onion to a medium bowl and stir in the bread crumbs and cilantro. Add the egg, salt and pepper and mix together well.

Divide the stuffing among the trout fillets, pressing it down well. Fold each fillet over to enclose the stuffing.

Arrange the fillets in greased dish. Sprinkle with the lemon juice and peel. Cover and bake 20 to 30 minutes, basting occasionally, until fish flakes when pierced with a fork. Serve with new potatoes and freshly cooked vegetables.

Makes 4 servings.

Each serving contains:				*Exchanges*:	
Calories	280	Total Fat	12g	Bread	0.4
Protein	32g	Saturated Fat	3g	Vegetable	0.4
Carbohydrates	9g	Cholesterol	139mg	Meat	4.2
Fiber	1g	Sodium	294mg	Fat	0.8

Pepper, Corn and Smoked-fish Stir-fry

*Late-Summer
Celebration Lunch*

*Broiled Salmon with Garlic
and Peppercorns
(page 49),*

*Creamy Leek and Ham
Tart (page 76) served
with boiled new potatoes
and a green salad or
freshly cooked broccoli,*

*Clafouti (page 172) made
with small, halved
plums, if cherries are
unavailable.*

Smoked fish has a strong flavor that is not to every-one's taste. However, this stir-fry uses lots of fresh vegetables and only a small amount of fish per serving, which may persuade any reluctant fish eaters in your household.

1	tablespoon olive or sunflower oil
1	small onion, thinly sliced
1	garlic clove, crushed
1	red bell pepper, seeded and sliced
1	green bell pepper, seeded and sliced
4	oz. baby sweet corn, sliced into large pieces
8	oz. skinned smoked-fish fillet, such as trout, or mackerel, sliced
8	oz. bean sprouts
1/4	cup dry sherry or red wine
	Freshly ground black pepper
	Cooked brown rice or noodles

Heat the oil in a large skillet or wok over high heat. Add the onion and garlic and cook 2 to 3 minutes, stirring. Stir in the bell peppers and baby corn and stir-fry another 2 minutes. Stir in the smoked fish and stir-fry 4 minutes, stirring carefully.

Add the bean sprouts, sherry, salt and pepper and cook another 2 minutes. Serve immediately with brown rice or noodles.

Makes 4 servings.

Each serving contains:

				Exchanges:	
Calories	199	Total Fat	12g	Bread	0.1
Protein	14g	Saturated Fat	2g	Vegetable	1.3
Carbohydrates	9g	Cholesterol	40mg	Meat	2.0
Fiber	3g	Sodium	61mg	Fat	0.9

Broiled Salmon with Garlic and Peppercorns

This salmon dish is marinated in advance and takes very little time to cook. That makes it just perfect for entertaining friends, especially if you are like me and don't like missing out on the conversation while you are busy in the kitchen!

	Juice of 1 lemon
2	garlic cloves, crushed
1/2	cup dry white wine
1	tablespoon crushed mixed peppercorns
6	(6-oz.) salmon steaks
2	lemons, sliced

Mix the lemon juice, garlic, wine and peppercorns together in a shallow nonaluminum ovenproof baking dish. Place the salmon steaks in the lemon juice mixture and turn to coat. Arrange half of the lemon slices on top of the steaks, cover and marinate in the refrigerator 2 hours or overnight.

Preheat broiler. Remove the lemon slices and broil the salmon steaks in the dish 4 to 5 minutes on each side, basting with the marinade mixture during cooking. Serve garnished with the remaining lemon slices.

Makes 6 servings.

Each serving contains:

				Exchanges:	
Calories	326	Total Fat	13g	Meat	6.0
Protein	47g	Saturated Fat	3g	Fat	0.3
Carbohydrates	0g	Cholesterol	97mg		
Fiber	0g	Sodium	91mg		

Fresh Herb-and-Shrimp Omelet

Summer Lunch for Two

Fresh Herb-and-Shrimp Omelet (opposite) served with Tomato and Red Onion Salad (page 58) and slices from warm Whole-wheat Bread loaf (page 123)

Fresh fruit to finish

A light, tasty omelet that is ideal for summer when fresh herbs are in abundance in the garden. If your green thumb fails you, many supermarkets sell packages of fresh herbs. If all else fails, substitute dried herbs in place of fresh. You will need about 1 teaspoon of dried herbs to replace the fresh herbs in the recipe.

4	eggs, beaten
	Salt and freshly ground black pepper
2	tablespoons nonfat milk
1	tablespoon olive or sunflower oil
3	oz. peeled cooked small shrimp, thawed if frozen
1	tablespoon fresh chopped herbs such as parsley or tarragon

Whisk together the eggs, salt, pepper and milk. Heat the oil in a medium nonstick skillet over medium heat. Add egg mixture and cook until lightly set. Sprinkle the shrimp and herbs over the eggs and cook 2 to 3 minutes to heat through. Fold in half and serve immediately. Serve with a tossed green salad and crusty bread.

Makes 2 servings.

Each serving contains:

Calories	256	Total Fat	17g		
Protein	22g	Saturated Fat	4g		
Carbohydrates	2g	Cholesterol	508mg		
Fiber	0g	Sodium	496mg		

Exchanges:

Milk	0.1
Meat	2.7
Fat	2.3

Crispy Baked Fish

A simple dish that is quick to prepare and to cook, ideal for a weekday meal. Serve with baked potatoes and freshly cooked vegetables.

4	fish fillets (6 oz. each), skinned
2 to 3	tablespoons lemon juice
	Salt and freshly ground black pepper
1	oz. (about 1/4 cup) shredded reduced-fat Cheddar cheese
3/4	cup fresh whole-wheat bread crumbs

Preheat oven to 375F (190C). Lay the fillets skinned side up on a board. Sprinkle each fillet with a little lemon juice, salt and pepper. Roll up the fillets from head to tail and place in an ovenproof dish. Secure with a wooden pick if necessary. Cover and bake 25 to 30 minutes or until fish changes from translucent to opaque.

Mix the cheese and bread crumbs together. Remove the cover from the fish and spoon the cheese mixture over the top. Return to the oven 5 minutes or until the topping is crisp and golden brown.

Makes 4 servings.

Each serving contains:

Calories	250	Total Fat	3g	Bread	0.6
Protein	44g	Saturated Fat	1g	Meat	3.5
Carbohydrates	10g	Cholesterol	123mg		
Fiber	1g	Sodium	377mg		

Exchanges:

Tuna-and-Cheese Sandwiches

The addition of shredded cheese adds both flavor and color to my tuna sandwiches.

1	(7-oz.) can tuna packed in water, drained and flaked
1	oz. (about 1/4 cup) shredded reduced-fat Cheddar cheese
1	stalk celery, finely chopped
3	tablespoons reduced-calorie salad dressing
8	slices whole-wheat bread

Mix the tuna, cheese, celery and salad dressing together in a bowl. Spread on 4 slices of bread and top with remaining slices.

Makes 4 sandwiches.

Each serving contains:

Calories	281	Total Fat	7g		
Protein	22g	Saturated Fat	2g		
Carbohydrates	35g	Cholesterol	25mg		
Fiber	4g	Sodium	648mg		

Exchanges:

Bread	2.3
Vegetable	0.1
Meat	1.5
Fat	0.4

Vegetarian

For the growing number of vegetarians, this section includes a variety of main-course recipes, as well as fresh salads and vegetable side dishes. I have included lots of legumes that contain soluble fiber, such as beans and lentils. Soluble fiber can help control blood-glucose levels by slowing down the rate at which sugars in foods get into the blood. It may also help reduce the amount of cholesterol in the blood. I enjoy vegetarian food and quite often choose the vegetarian option when dining out. I particularly like the spicy recipes in this section.

Mediterranean Gougère

I often use a food processor to add the eggs to the dough mixture to obtain a smooth, glossy result. Use a slotted spoon when adding the vegetables to the pastry ring so that the filling is not too runny.

5	tablespoons soft margarine
1	cup cold water
1	cup all-purpose flour
1/2	teaspoon salt
3	eggs, beaten
3	oz. (about 3/4 cup) shredded reduced-fat Cheddar cheese
1	tablespoon olive or sunflower oil
1	small onion, finely diced
2	garlic cloves, crushed
1	green bell pepper, seeded and diced
1	red bell pepper, seeded and diced
2	small zucchini, sliced
1	(14-oz.) can chopped tomatoes, drained
1	tablespoon chopped fresh mixed herbs
	Salt and freshly ground black pepper

The cooked pastry ring can be frozen if you leave it unfilled. Cool, split horizontally and put a sheet of waxed paper between the halves. Pack into a rigid container. Thaw before filling.

Preheat oven to 425F (220C). Place the margarine and water in a saucepan over medium heat. Bring to a boil, remove from the heat and add the flour and salt all at once. Beat well 1 to 2 minutes, or until the mixture forms a ball and leaves the sides of the pan clean. Allow to cool slightly. Gradually add the eggs, a little at a time, beating until the mixture is smooth, thick and glossy. Beat in half the cheese. Draw an 8-inch circle on a sheet of parchment paper and place paper on a baking sheet.

Spoon or pipe the dough onto the paper to form a circle.

Bake 20 minutes. Reduce the heat to 375F (190C) and bake 10 minutes or until puffed and golden. Carefully remove the paper and cool on a wire rack.

Meanwhile, heat the oil in a medium saucepan. Add the onion and garlic and cook 2 to 3 minutes or until soft, stirring occasionally. Add the bell peppers, cover and cook over low heat 5 minutes. Stir in the zucchini, tomatoes and herbs. Cook, uncovered, 15 minutes or until the vegetables are tender. Season with salt and pepper and remove from the heat.

Split the pastry ring in half horizontally. Place the bottom half on a baking sheet. With a slotted spoon, arrange vegetables in the bottom ring and cover with the top. Sprinkle with the remaining cheese and return to the oven 5 minutes to heat through. Serve immediately with steamed broccoli and a mixed green salad.

Makes 6 servings.

Each serving contains:				*Exchanges*:	
Calories	268	Total Fat	16g	Bread	0.9
Protein	10g	Saturated Fat	3g	Vegetable	1.1
Carbohydrates	22g	Cholesterol	109mg	Meat	0.9
Fiber	2g	Sodium	498mg	Fat	2.6

Easy Bean Salad

I prefer to use flat-leaf or Italian parsley for the dressing. Its flavor is more distinctive than curly parsley.

Dressing beans well in advance enables them to absorb all flavors fully, but if you dress salad greens too far in advance, they become soft and lose their crunch. If you need to display the food in advance (for example, in a buffet), serve the bean salad in a small dish set among the green leaves.

5	oz. green beans, trimmed and cut into small pieces
1	(15-oz.) can red kidney beans, rinsed and drained
1	(15-oz.) can Great Northern beans, rinsed and drained
1	(15-oz.) can chickpeas, rinsed and drained
2	tablespoons fresh parsley, chopped
	Juice of 1 lemon
2	tablespoons white-wine vinegar
5	tablespoons olive oil
	Freshly ground black pepper
	Lettuce leaves to garnish

Lightly steam the green beans over boiling water 5 to 6 minutes or until crisp-tender. Cool in iced water and drain. Place in a large bowl with the kidney beans, Great Northern beans and chickpeas and mix well.

In a jar with a tight-fitting lid, shake together the parsley, lemon juice, vinegar, olive oil and pepper. Pour over the bean mixture and toss lightly to mix. Cover and chill until served.

Just before serving, place the lettuce leaves around the edge of a large serving dish. Spoon the bean mixture over the leaves and serve.

Makes 6 to 8 side-salad servings.

Each serving contains:				*Exchanges*:	
Calories	397	Total Fat	14g	Bread	3.0
Protein	19g	Saturated Fat	2g	Vegetable	0.2
Carbohydrates	52g	Cholesterol	0mg	Meat	1.3
Fiber	14g	Sodium	9mg	Fat	2.2

Greek Salad

This is my favorite dish for a simple lunch with crusty bread. It can also be served as a side salad, serving four. If you are watching calories, omit the oil and save 200 calories in the dish.

Feta cheese is traditionally made from sheep's milk but now is often made from cow's milk. It is usually available in the cheese section of most supermarkets and delicatessens.

1/2	head iceberg lettuce, coarsely chopped
1/2	cucumber, diced
2	beefsteak tomatoes, sliced
3	oz. feta cheese, crumbled
8	ripe Greek olives, pitted
2	tablespoons olive oil
	Freshly ground black pepper

Arrange the lettuce, cucumber, tomatoes, cheese and olives on 2 serving dishes. Drizzle with the oil and season with black pepper to taste.

Makes 2 main-dish servings or 4 side-salad servings.

Each main-dish serving contains:

Calories	375	Total Fat	28g
Protein	12g	Saturated Fat	10g
Carbohydrates	23g	Cholesterol	38mg
Fiber	6g	Sodium	1055mg

Exchanges:

Vegetable	2.5
Fat	3.7

Tomato and Red Onion Salad

Beefsteak tomatoes are extra large and sometimes have an irregular shape. They are particularly good in salads because of their firm texture. The red onion and full-flavored dressing in this salad add extra flavor.

Balsamic vinegar is a rich, sweet-sour vinegar that has become very popular for cooking as well as on salads. Find it in delicatessens and most larger supermarkets.

3	tablespoons olive oil
1	tablespoon balsamic vinegar
	Salt and freshly ground black pepper
1-1/2	lb. beefsteak or large tomatoes, sliced
2	medium red onions, peeled and sliced
	Finely chopped fresh chives to garnish

Whisk together the oil, vinegar, salt and pepper in a large bowl. Add the tomatoes and onions and toss in the olive oil mixture. Place in a serving bowl and let marinate in the refrigerator 30 minutes before serving. Garnish with chopped fresh chives.

Makes 4 to 6 servings.

Each serving contains:

Calories	146	Total Fat	11g	Vegetable	2.1
Protein	2g	Saturated Fat	1g	Fat	2.0
Carbohydrates	13g	Cholesterol	0mg		
Fiber	3g	Sodium	150mg		

Exchanges:

Light Salad Niçoise

Salad Niçoise can be quite high in fat. I've reduced the fat content by using canned tuna in water and fat-free dressing. Both products are readily available in supermarkets. Serve with fresh crusty bread.

1	head iceberg lettuce, finely shredded
2	large beefsteak tomatoes, cut into wedges
3	oz. green beans, cooked and cooled
6	green onions, sliced
1	garlic clove, crushed
1/4	cup fat-free vinaigrette dressing
2	(7-oz.) cans tuna in water, drained
6	anchovy fillets, drained
8	ripe Greek olives, pitted
4	hard-cooked eggs, quartered

Place the lettuce, tomatoes, beans and onions in a serving bowl and toss lightly together. Mix the garlic into the dressing and drizzle half of it over the contents of the bowl. Add the tuna in large chunks. Pat the anchovy fillets dry on paper towels and place on top of the tuna with the olives. Drizzle with the remaining dressing and arrange the eggs on top of the salad. Serve chilled.

Makes 4 servings.

Vary the ingredients in this salad with sliced cucumber, strips of green pepper, tiny fresh green beans or, for a treat, add a can of drained and quartered artichoke hearts. Artichokes are high in iron and potassium, low in fat and boast fewer than 16 calories per ounce (25g). The carbohydrate value is negligible.

Each serving contains:

Calories	297	Total Fat	10g	Vegetable	1.1
Protein	37g	Saturated Fat	3g	Meat	3.7
Carbohydrates	15g	Cholesterol	259mg	Fat	0.7
Fiber	4g	Sodium	955mg		

Exchanges:

Black-eyed Pea and Spinach Omelet

Pack a Picnic for Two

*Black-eyed Pea and
    Spinach Omelet
    (opposite) served with
    crusty bread, cherry
    tomatoes and slices of
    cucumber.*

Carrot Cake (page 128)

Fresh fruit

This is a great addition to a picnic basket, in place of the more typical sandwiches or as a quick dish for a light supper or lunch. Serve with a side salad and fresh crusty bread.

1	tablespoon olive or sunflower oil
1	red onion, thinly sliced
2	garlic cloves, crushed
1	teaspoon ground turmeric
1	(15-oz.) can black-eyed peas, drained
1	(10-oz.) pkg. frozen leaf spinach, thawed and squeezed dry
4	eggs
	Salt and freshly ground black pepper

Preheat broiler. Heat the oil in a large nonstick skillet with a ovenproof handle over medium heat. Add the onion, garlic and turmeric and cook, stirring occasionally, 4 to 5 minutes. Stir in the peas and spinach.

Whisk the eggs, salt and pepper together and stir into the pan to coat the other ingredients thoroughly. Cook 6 to 7 minutes or until nearly set.

Broil 2 to 3 minutes or until the omelet is set on top. Cut into wedges and serve hot or cold.

Makes 2 servings.

Each serving contains:

				Exchanges:	
Calories	550	Total Fat	19g	Bread	3.2
Protein	36g	Saturated Fat	4g	Vegetable	3.6
Carbohydrates	64g	Cholesterol	425mg	Meat	1.9
Fiber	23g	Sodium	527mg	Fat	2.3

Chickpea, Apricot and Cashew Pilaf

A filling dish that features a lovely combination of textures from the rice, chickpeas and cashews. It is a good source of fiber.

Serve with Tomato and Red Onion Salad (page 58).

1	tablespoon olive or sunflower oil
1	large onion, finely chopped
2	garlic cloves, crushed
1	large carrot, diced
1	teaspoon ground cumin
1/2	teaspoon ground cinnamon
1	cup brown rice
2-1/2	cups vegetable stock
1	(15-oz.) can chickpeas, drained
2	oz. dried apricots, chopped
3	oz. unsalted cashew nuts
2	tablespoons chopped fresh cilantro
	Salt and freshly ground black pepper

Heat the oil in a large nonstick skillet or saucepan over medium heat. Add the onion, garlic and carrot and cook, stirring occasionally, 5 minutes or until soft and golden. Stir in the cumin, cinnamon and rice and cook 1 minute, stirring.

Stir in the stock, bring to a boil. Reduce heat, cover and simmer 40 minutes. Stir in the chickpeas, apricots, cashews, cilantro, salt and pepper. Cook, uncovered, 5 to 10 minutes or until all the liquid has been absorbed. Serve hot.

Makes 4 servings.

Exchanges:

Bread	4.1
Vegetable	1.0
Fruit	0.6
Meat	0.9
Fat	1.9

Each serving contains:

Calories	570	Total Fat	18g
Protein	18g	Saturated Fat	3g
Carbohydrates	90g	Cholesterol	0mg
Fiber	11g	Sodium	164mg

Zucchini, Baby Corn and Red Pepper Pizza

Quick-rise Yeast

This quick form of yeast is added to the dry ingredients, not mixed with water first, and the water has to be slightly warmer than for conventional yeast. If you have regular yeast, add it to 1/4 cup warm water (110F/53C) in a small bowl. Add a pinch of sugar and let stand until foamy, about 5 minutes. Add the remaining water with the oil.

I use a heavy-duty or stand electric mixer to knead the dough, which only takes 12 minutes. The dough is enough to make two thin 9-inch pizzas.

For the base

1	cup all-purpose flour
1/2	cup whole-wheat flour
1/4	teaspoon salt
1/2	cup warm water (125 to 130F/63C), about
1	tablespoon olive or sunflower oil

Topping

1	tablespoon olive or sunflower oil
1	red onion, sliced
2	large zucchini, sliced
4	oz. canned baby corn, drained and sliced
2	red bell peppers, diced
2	(14-oz.) cans chopped tomatoes, drained
1	tablespoon tomato paste
2	tablespoons chopped fresh basil
1-1/2	cup (6 oz.) shredded vegetarian cheddar cheese
12	ripe olives in brine, pitted
5 to 6	fresh basil leaves

Add the flours into a large bowl. Stir in the yeast and salt. Make a well in the center and gradually work in the water and oil to form a soft dough. Knead on a lightly floured surface for 8 to 10 minutes or until smooth and elastic. Place in an oiled bowl, cover and let rise in a warm place 45 minutes or until doubled in size.

Meanwhile, heat the oil in a medium saucepan. Add the onion, zucchini, baby corn and peppers and stir-fry 2 to 3 minutes. Remove from the heat and set aside. Preheat the oven to 450F (230C). Place a large baking sheet on the top shelf of the oven. Knead the risen dough on a lightly floured surface. Roll out into two 9-inch rounds and press into pizza pans or shallow cake pans.

Mix the drained tomatoes with the tomato paste and chopped basil and spread over the pizza bases, almost to the edge. Top with the cooked vegetables and sprinkle with cheese, olives and basil leaves.

Place the pizzas on the preheated baking sheet in the oven and cook for 20 to 25 minutes until the top is bubbling and golden. Serve at once. Makes two 9-inch pizzas for 4 servings.

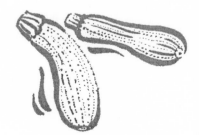

Each serving contains:				*Exchanges*:	
Calories	386	Total Fat	10g	Bread	2.0
Protein	18g	Saturated Fat	1g	Vegetable	3.0
Carbohydrates	59g	Cholesterol	6mg	Fat	1.6
Fiber	7g	Sodium	1264mg		

Spicy Cajun Casserole

A filling casserole with a spicy punch! The heat of the chili really brings out the sweetness of the root vegetables. Serve as a main meal with fresh crusty bread or alternatively, serve in smaller portions as a side vegetable.

This casserole is suitable for freezing. Thaw completely in the refrigerator and then reheat in a saucepan. Simmer 10 minutes or until piping hot, adding a little extra water or stock if the mixture becomes too dry.

1	tablespoon olive or sunflower oil
2	medium onions, finely diced
2	garlic cloves, crushed
3	small carrots, sliced
2	medium parsnips, diced
8	oz. button mushrooms, halved
1	green bell pepper, seeded and chopped
1 to 2	teaspoons chili powder
1	tablespoon tomato paste
1-1/2	cups vegetable stock
1	(14-oz.) can chopped tomatoes
1	(15-oz.) can black-eyed peas, drained
2	teaspoons dried mixed herbs
	A few drops hot-pepper sauce

Heat the oil in a large saucepan over medium heat. Add the onions and garlic and cook 2 to 3 minutes, stirring. Add the carrots, parsnips, mushrooms and bell pepper and cook another 5 minutes, stirring occasionally. Stir in the chili powder and tomato paste and gradually stir in the stock. Add the remaining ingredients and bring to a boil. Reduce heat, cover and simmer 40 to 50 minutes or until vegetables are tender.

Makes 4 to 6 servings.

Each serving contains:

Calories	313	Total Fat	5g	Bread	2.2
Protein	14g	Saturated Fat	1g	Vegetable	3.7
Carbohydrates	58g	Cholesterol	0mg	Fat	0.7
Fiber	17g	Sodium	228mg		

Exchanges:

Risotto Primavera

This recipe is high in complex carbohydrates and low in fat. For a nonvegetarian meal, add chopped cooked pork, beef or chicken at the same time you add the vegetables.

1	tablespoon olive or sunflower oil
1	onion, finely chopped
2	carrots, diced
2	medium zucchini, diced
4	oz. baby corn, sliced into small pieces
3	stalks celery, sliced
1-1/2	cups brown rice
2	teaspoons dried mixed herbs
4	cups vegetable stock
1	large tomato, peeled and chopped
	Salt and freshly ground black pepper
1	tablespoon chopped fresh parsley

Heat the oil in a heavy saucepan over medium heat. Add the onion, carrots, zucchini, baby corn and celery and cook 5 minutes or until just soft. Stir in the rice and herbs and cook 1 to 2 minutes, stirring constantly. Gradually stir in the stock, cover and simmer 45 to 50 minutes or until all the stock has been absorbed. Stir in the tomato and cook 5 minutes. Season with salt and pepper and serve hot, garnished with chopped fresh parsley. Serve with a crisp salad.

Makes 4 to 6 servings.

The word primavera *is added to a dish to mean "with fresh spring vegetables", presumably from the word* primeurs, *meaning "early forced vegetable and fruit".*

Spring Lunch

Quick Tomato Salsa with tortilla chips (page 30)

Risotto Primavera served with a crisp salad of finely shredded spring greens

Rhubarb-and-Ginger Fool (page 151)

Each serving contains:

Calories	365	Total Fat	6g	Bread	3.5
Protein	8g	Saturated Fat	1g	Vegetable	2.0
Carbohydrates	71g	Cholesterol	0mg	Fat	0.7
Fiber	7g	Sodium	199mg		

Exchanges:

Creamy Curried Potato Salad

Serve as part of a buffet lunch with roasted chicken drumsticks, cherry tomatoes or Tomato and Red Onion Salad (page 58), light coleslaw, Easy Bean Salad (page 56) and wedges of crisp lettuce. Finish with Spiced Mandarin Gâteau (page 130).

Keep the skin on the potatoes to retain valuable vitamins and fiber. Stir in the dressing while the potatoes are warm so the dressing is absorbed.

1-1/2	lb. baby new potatoes, scrubbed
1/3	cup fat-free sour cream
1/3	cup fat-free mayonnaise
1/4	teaspoon ground coriander
1/4	teaspoon ground cumin
	Salt and freshly ground black pepper
2	tablespoons chopped fresh chives

Cook the potatoes in boiling water until tender. Meanwhile, whisk together the sour cream, mayonnaise, coriander, cumin, salt and pepper in a large bowl. Drain the potatoes and immediately stir into the dressing. Cover and refrigerate.

Just before serving, stir in the chives. Best eaten the same day.

Makes 8 to 10 servings.

Each serving contains:

				Exchanges:	
Calories	91	Total Fat	0g	Bread	0.9
Protein	2g	Saturated Fat	0g		
Carbohydrates	20g	Cholesterol	0mg		
Fiber	2g	Sodium	147mg		

Eastern Spiced Vegetables

As a side dish, these spiced vegetables go very well with the Marinated Chicken and Rosemary Kebabs (page 98).

I am very fond of vegetable curries and will often choose one when we have an Indian meal. This recipe can also be used as a side dish. Vary the vegetables to suit your taste or what you have on hand.

1	tablespoon olive or corn oil
1	large onion, sliced
1	tablespoon curry powder
2	teaspoons chili powder
1	teaspoon ground turmeric
1	green bell pepper, seeded and chopped
2	garlic cloves, crushed
3	small zucchini, sliced
2	large carrots, diced
4	oz. baby corn, sliced into small pieces
8	oz. cauliflower, cut into small florets
1	(15-oz.) can chickpeas, drained
1	(14-oz.) can chopped tomatoes
1/2	cup water
	Salt and freshly ground black pepper

Heat the oil in a large skillet or wok over medium heat. Add the onion, curry powder, chili powder and turmeric and cook 1 to 2 minutes, stirring constantly. Stir in the remaining ingredients, bring to a boil. Reduce heat, half cover and simmer 20 minutes or until the liquid is absorbed.

Makes 4 to 6 servings.

Each serving contains:

				Exchanges:	
Calories	284	Total Fat	7g	Bread	2.0
Protein	13g	Saturated Fat	1g	Vegetable	2.7
Carbohydrates	46g	Cholesterol	0mg	Meat	0.5
Fiber	10g	Sodium	338mg	Fat	0.7

Chili-Bean Enchiladas

Whole-wheat flour tortillas, made with vegetable shortening instead of lard, are available in many supermarkets and health-food stores.

8	whole-wheat tortillas
1	(15-oz.) can vegetarian refried beans
1	(15-oz.) can pinto beans, rinsed and drained
1	to 2 teaspoons hot chili powder
1	teaspoon ground cumin
3	oz. (about 3/4 cup) shredded reduced-fat Cheddar cheese

Preheat oven to 400F (205C). Heat a skillet over medium heat and warm each tortilla and keep warm in a damp towel. Mix together the beans, chili powder and cumin in a medium bowl. Divide the beans among the tortillas, sprinkle with cheese and roll up. Place in an ovenproof dish. Bake 20 minutes or until centers are hot. Serve with salsa and a green salad.

Makes 4 servings.

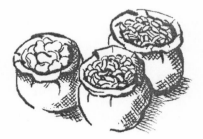

Each serving contains:

Calories	363	Total Fat	4g
Protein	22g	Saturated Fat	1g
Carbohydrates	70g	Cholesterol	4mg
Fiber	15g	Sodium	993mg

Exchanges:

Bread	1.8
Meat	0.7

Bean Burgers

I use a dried-bean mixture available prepacked in my local supermarket. Remember the beans need to be prepared before cooking the burgers.

Cook dried beans in unsalted water until they are almost tender, because salt tends to toughen them. Add any salt about 15 minutes before the end of the cooking time.

6	oz. dried mixed beans, prepared as indicated below
1	tablespoon olive or sunflower oil plus oil for brushing
1	small onion, finely chopped
1	large carrot, grated
1	teaspoon dried mixed herbs
1	cup fresh whole-wheat bread crumbs
	Salt and freshly ground black pepper

Drain the soaked beans and rinse thoroughly. Place in a large saucepan and cover with cold water. Boil vigorously 10 minutes. Reduce the heat and simmer 1 hour or until the beans are soft. Drain well.

Meanwhile, heat the 1 tablespoon oil in a small pan over medium heat. Add the onion and cook until soft. Drain thoroughly on paper towels.

Combine the beans, onion and remaining ingredients in a food processor and process until almost smooth. Season with salt and pepper.

Using wet hands, shape the mixture into 6 burgers. Chill at least 30 minutes.

Preheat broiler. Brush the burgers with a little oil and broil about 15 minutes, turning once, or until heated through. Serve hot in toasted buns.

Makes 6 servings.

Each serving contains:

Calories	92	Total Fat	3g	*Exchanges*:	
Protein	4g	Saturated Fat	0g	Bread	0.6
Carbohydrates	14g	Cholesterol	0mg	Vegetable	0.3
Fiber	4g	Sodium	144mg	Meat	0.2
				Fat	0.4

Baked-Bean Lasagna

Use water instead of milk and a vegetarian cheese if you are a vegan.

A high-fiber recipe everyone will love.

1	tablespoon olive or sunflower oil
1	large onion, finely chopped
5	oz. mushrooms, sliced
1	(15-oz.) can baked beans
1	tablespoon tomato paste
1/2	cup vegetable stock
2	tablespoons soft margarine
2	tablespoons all-purpose flour
1	cup nonfat milk
	Salt and freshly ground black pepper
3	oz. (about 3/4 cup) shredded reduced-fat Cheddar cheese
6	to 8 sheets whole-wheat lasagna noodles, cooked

Preheat oven to 375F (190C). Heat the oil in a non-stick saucepan over medium heat. Add the onion and mushrooms and cook 5 minutes or until soft. Add the baked beans, tomato paste and stock and mix well. Set aside until required.

Melt the margarine in a saucepan, stir in the flour and cook for 1 minute, stirring. Gradually stir in the milk and cook, stirring constantly, until the sauce thickens. Season with salt and pepper and add half the cheese, stirring well to mix.

Spoon half the bean mixture over the bottom of a 9-inch square ovenproof dish. Cover with half the noodles. Repeat the layers, ending with noodles. Spoon the cheese sauce over the noodles. Top with the remaining cheese. Bake 25 to 30 minutes.

Makes 4 to 6 servings.

For 4 servings, each serving contains:

				Exchanges:	
Calories	440	Total Fat	12g	Bread	3.5
Protein	20g	Saturated Fat	3g	Vegetable	1.1
Carbohydrates	67g	Cholesterol	6mg	Meat	0.6
Fiber	9g	Sodium	681mg	Fat	2.0

Meat

I've used a variety of meats and a lot of poultry recipes. The emphasis is on Mediterranean flavors and includes dishes such as kebabs and pasta dishes, but there are some traditional hearty stews—like Beef Burgundy—and casseroles with beer or dumplings, too. Also included are stir-fry recipes; you'll find Ham-and-Pineapple Stir-fry appeals to the eye as well as the palate.

Beef Casserole with Herb Dumplings

Winter Supper for Four

Beef Casserole with Herb Dumplings (opposite) served with new potatoes and steamed wedges of cabbage or Brussels sprouts

Pears with Raspberry Sauce (page 156)

Long, slow cooking ensures that the meat is tender. The vegetables add rich flavor.

1	lb. lean beef round steak, fat removed and cubed
8	oz. rutabaga, peeled and diced
8	oz. boiling onions or shallots, peeled
5	oz. button mushrooms, halved
2	large carrots, sliced
1	bouquet garni
2	cups beef stock
1	tablespoon Worcestershire sauce
	Salt and freshly ground black pepper

Herb Dumplings

1/2	cup whole-wheat flour
1/2	cup all-purpose flour
1	teaspoon baking powder
1/2	teaspoon salt
2	teaspoons dried Italian seasoning
3	tablespoons vegetable oil spread
1/2	cup nonfat milk, about

Preheat oven to 350F (175C). Place the steak, vegetables, bouquet garni, stock and Worcestershire sauce in a Dutch oven or large ovenproof casserole dish. Season with salt and pepper. Bring to a boil over medium heat. Cover and bake 1 hour, stirring occasionally.

In a small bowl, mix together all the ingredients for the dumplings, adding enough milk to form a stiff batter. Drop 8 spoonfuls of batter into casserole.

Bake 1 hour. Remove the bouquet garni before serving. Serve with new potatoes and cooked vegetables.

Makes 4 servings.

Each serving contains:

					Exchanges:	
Calories	481	Total Fat	17g		Bread	1.3
Protein	42g	Saturated Fat	4g		Vegetable	2.5
Carbohydrates	41g	Cholesterol	79mg		Milk	0.1
Fiber	5g	Sodium	758mg		Meat	4.0
					Fat	1.7

Lentil Hot Pot

Using legumes such as lentils adds extra fiber to casserole dishes and also gives a meaty taste to the dish so less meat is required.

Lentils are low in fat and a good source of protein. Unlike most dried legumes, they do not require soaking overnight before use.

2	tablespoons all-purpose flour
	Salt and freshly ground black pepper
2	teaspoons dried rosemary
1-1/4	lb. lean lamb or beef cubes, fat removed
2/3	cup red lentils
1	large onion, finely diced
2	carrots, sliced
12	oz. rutabagas, diced
2-1/2	cups beef stock
1-1/2	lb. (about 4 medium) potatoes
1	tablespoon olive or corn oil

The hot pot has had a checkered history. Originally it was a boiled mixture of ale and spirits (usually brandy), but by the middle of the nineteenth century it had become a dish of meat and vegetables topped with potatoes. Different meats have been included over the years. For a change, try lean pork, adding a few apple slices under the potato.

Preheat oven to 325F (165C). Season the flour with the salt, pepper and rosemary. Toss the lamb or beef in the flour to coat evenly. Place in a Dutch oven or ovenproof casserole dish.

Boil the lentils in boiling water 10 minutes. Drain and rinse. Add to the casserole dish with the onion, carrot, rutabaga and stock. Mix well. Bring to a boil over medium heat. Cover and bake 1-1/2 hours. Peel and thinly slice the potatoes. Cover top of the casserole with potatoes and brush with oil.

Return to the oven and bake, uncovered, 1 hour or until potatoes are tender. Serve hot with cooked green vegetables.

Makes 4 servings.

Each serving contains:

				Exchanges:	
Calories	715	Total Fat	21g	Bread	3.3
Protein	61g	Saturated Fat	7g	Vegetable	2.2
Carbohydrates	70g	Cholesterol	144mg	Meat	6.2
Fiber	10g	Sodium	643mg	Fat	0.7

Beef Burgundy

A classic Burgundy dish. The flavor improves if it is made a day in advance and kept in the refrigerator.

If you make Beef Burgundy ahead, refrigerate it. Then remove any fat that rises to the top and hardens before you reheat the dish.

2	tablespoons olive oil
2	lb. lean round steak, cubed
2	slices lean bacon, finely chopped
3	stalks celery, sliced
4	carrots, sliced
2	garlic cloves, crushed
1	tablespoon all-purpose flour
2	cups beef stock
1/2	cup dry red wine
1	bay leaf
1	bouquet garni
	Salt and freshly ground black pepper
12	boiling onions, peeled

Preheat oven to 350F (175C). Heat the oil in a large pan over medium heat. Add beef a few pieces at a time and cook until browned. Drain and transfer to a large casserole dish. Add the bacon, celery, carrots and garlic to the pan and cook 2 minutes.

Stir the flour into the pan and cook 1 minute, stirring constantly. Gradually add the stock, wine, bay leaf, bouquet garni, salt and pepper. Bring to a boil and pour over the meat. Cover and bake 2 hours. Stir in the onions and bake 30 minutes or until onions and beef are tender. Remove the bouquet garni and bay leaf and adjust seasoning if necessary.

Makes 6 or 8 servings.

For 6 people, each serving contains:

				Exchanges:	
Calories	400	Total Fat	14g	Bread	0.1
Protein	52g	Saturated Fat	4g	Vegetable	1.7
Carbohydrates	12g	Cholesterol	129mg	Meat	5.1
Fiber	2g	Sodium	279mg	Fat	1.3

Creamy Leek and Ham Tart

A delicious, creamy tart that may be eaten hot or cold. Take this to your next picnic; it's a nice change from sandwiches.

Pastry

1	cup whole-wheat flour
3/4	cup all-purpose flour
	Pinch of salt
1/2	cup vegetable-oil spread
	About 3 tablespoons water

Leek and Ham Filling

8	oz. leeks, sliced lengthwise, rinsed well and thinly · sliced crosswise
1-1/2	cups nonfat milk
3	tablespoons all-purpose flour
2	tablespoons vegetable-oil spread
2	oz. (about 1/2 cup) shredded reduced-fat Cheddar cheese
2	eggs, beaten
2	oz. lean ham, chopped
	Freshly ground black pepper

Sift the flours into a bowl. Add any bran remaining in the sifter to the bowl. Cut in the fats until the mixture resembles fine bread crumbs. Add enough cold water to mix to a soft dough. Shape into a ball, cover, and refrigerate 10 minutes.

Preheat oven to 400F (205C). Roll out dough on a lightly floured board to an 11-inch circle. Use to line a 9-inch tart pan. Line pastry with foil and add about 1-1/2 cups dried beans. Bake 10 minutes. Remove the beans and foil and bake 5 minutes. Remove from oven and reduce temperature to 375F (190C).

Cook the leeks in boiling water 10 minutes or until tender. Drain well and set aside.

In a saucepan, whisk a little of the milk with the flour. Add remaining milk and vegetable spread. Bring to a boil over medium heat, whisking constantly. Cook, whisking constantly, 1 to 2 minutes or until thickened. Remove from the heat and add a little of the hot mixture to the eggs. Return to saucepan with the cheese. Whisk together until smooth. Season with pepper. Fold in the leeks and ham. Spoon into the cooked pastry shell. Bake 35 to 40 minutes or until golden. Cool slightly before cutting into wedges.

Makes 8 servings.

Each serving contains:

Calories	296	Total Fat	17g		
Protein	10g	Saturated Fat	3g		
Carbohydrates	27g	Cholesterol	59mg		
Fiber	3g	Sodium	310mg		

Exchanges:

Bread	1.3
Vegetable	0.3
Meat	0.6
Fat	3.0

Round Steak with Spicy Tomato Sauce

A simple, economical meal that tastes great. Serve with potatoes and freshly cooked vegetables.

1	tablespoon all-purpose flour
	Salt and freshly ground black pepper
1-1/4	lb. lean beef round steak, thinly sliced
2	tablespoons olive or sunflower oil
1	large onion, thinly sliced
3	stalks celery, thinly sliced
1	teaspoon paprika
1	(14-oz.) can chopped tomatoes

Season flour with salt and pepper. Dust the beef with the seasoned flour. Heat the oil in a nonstick deep skillet over medium heat. Add the beef, turning to brown both sides. Add the onion, celery, paprika and tomatoes. Cover and simmer over low heat until beef and vegetables are tender, 30 to 40 minutes. Serve hot.

Makes 4 servings.

Each serving contains:

				Exchanges:	
Calories	354	Total Fat	15g	Bread	0.1
Protein	43g	Saturated Fat	4g	Vegetable	1.5
Carbohydrates	10g	Cholesterol	98mg	Meat	5.0
Fiber	2g	Sodium	410mg	Fat	1.3

Thirty-minute Meatballs

If you can't find fresh oregano, use 2 teaspoons of dried oregano instead. Chop the onion very finely or the mixture will be difficult to form into balls.

Thirty-minute Supper

Quick Chickpea Dip served
   with vegetable crudités
   (page 28)

Thirty-minute Meatballs
   (opposite) served with
   pasta

Peach Yogurt Crunch
   (page 165)

1	lb. extra-lean ground beef
1	onion, very finely chopped
2	tablespoons chopped fresh oregano
	Salt and freshly ground black pepper
2	garlic cloves, crushed
1	cup canned crushed plum tomatoes in purée
1/2	cup dry red wine
1	red bell pepper, seeded and finely chopped
1	green bell pepper, seeded and finely chopped

Mix the beef, onion, oregano, salt and pepper together in a large bowl. With your wet hands, shape the mixture into about 16 balls. Chill in the refrigerator until required.

Place the remaining ingredients in a large saucepan and simmer 5 minutes. Add salt and pepper to taste. Add the meatballs, bring to a boil. Reduce heat, cover and simmer 20 minutes or until cooked through. Serve with cooked pasta.

Makes 4 servings.

Each serving contains:

				Exchanges:	
Calories	368	Total Fat	18g	Vegetable	1.9
Protein	34g	Saturated Fat	7g	Meat	4.0
Carbohydrates	12g	Cholesterol	112mg	Fat	1.8
Fiber	3g	Sodium	479mg		

Light Pastitsio

This is a spicy Greek dish. I have adapted it to reduce the fat content without affecting the flavor. Serve with a fresh green salad.

Pasta is usually thought of as an Italian dish, but before the fourth century, when Latin cookbooks record the word to mean "dough," it was a food used by the Greeks. Their word for it meant "barley porridge." Macaroni has been around since the sixteenth century. Macaroni is actually a Greek word meaning "food made from barley." This Greek pasta dish is, therefore, very much an ancient specialty.

1	lb. extra-lean ground beef
1	large onion, finely chopped
2	garlic cloves, crushed
1	teaspoon dried oregano
1	teaspoon dried thyme
1	bay leaf
1/2	teaspoon ground cinnamon
1	teaspoon ground cumin
	Pinch of ground ginger
	Pinch of grated nutmeg
1/2	cup dry white wine
1	(14-oz.) can chopped tomatoes
1	tablespoon tomato paste
	Salt and freshly ground black pepper
6	oz. whole-wheat pasta
2	tablespoons chopped fresh cilantro (optional)
2	tablespoons vegetable oil spread
3	tablespoons all-purpose flour
1-1/2	cups nonfat milk
1/2	cup (2 oz.) shredded reduced-fat Cheddar cheese
1	egg, beaten

Cook beef, onion and garlic in a large nonstick pan over medium heat 5 minutes or until browned, stirring to break up beef. Stir in the herbs and spices and cook another 5 minutes, stirring occasionally.

Stir in the wine, tomatoes, tomato paste, salt and pepper. Bring to a boil, half cover and simmer 30 minutes, stirring occasionally, until the sauce is thickened and well reduced.

Meanwhile, cook the pasta in boiling, salted water until tender. Drain and stir into the beef mixture with the chopped cilantro, if using. Spoon into a large, shallow 1-quart baking dish.

Preheat oven to 375F (190C). In a saucepan, whisk a little of the milk with the flour. Add remaining milk and vegetable spread. Bring to a boil over medium heat, whisking constantly. Cook, whisking constantly, 1 to 2 minutes or until thickened. Remove from the heat and add a little of the hot mixture to the eggs. Return to saucepan with the cheese. Whisk together until smooth. Season with salt and pepper. Pour over the beef mixture. Bake 35 to 40 minutes or until golden brown and bubbly. Serve hot with a green salad and crusty bread, if desired.

Makes 4 to 6 servings.

Each serving contains:				*Exchanges*:	
				Bread	2.0
Calories	649	Total Fat	27g	Vegetable	1.5
Protein	49g	Saturated Fat	10g	Milk	0.4
Carbohydrates	49g	Cholesterol	170mg	Meat	4.7
Fiber	6g	Sodium	543mg	Fat	2.9

Beef, Pepper and Baby Corn Stir-fry

Beef fillet is expensive, but in this recipe, you can buy the thin end piece because it is cut into strips. You may substitute flank steak for the fillet.

Asian Supper for Four

Cheese-and-Spinach Filo Triangles (page 36)

Beef, Pepper and Baby Corn Stir-fry (opposite), served with noodles or rice

Figs with Blackberry Sauce (page 162)

This recipe is ideal for entertaining, because most of the preparation can be done in advance, leaving you more time to spend with guests. I marinate the meat in the morning and prepare the vegetables just before the guests arrive.

1	lb. lean beef fillet, sliced into very thin strips
1	tablespoon cornstarch
2	tablespoons soy sauce
6	tablespoons dry red wine
3	tablespoons red-wine vinegar
	Salt and freshly ground black pepper
1	tablespoon olive or corn oil
1	onion, finely sliced
2	garlic cloves, crushed
1	(1-inch) piece fresh ginger, grated
3	stalks celery, finely sliced
1	red bell pepper, seeded and thinly sliced
1	green bell pepper, seeded and thinly sliced
8	oz. baby corn, cut into small pieces
4	oz. brown or white mushrooms, sliced

Place the beef in a bowl. Mix together the cornstarch, soy sauce, wine and vinegar, salt and pepper in a small bowl. Pour over the meat, stir well to coat, cover and marinate in the refrigerator 2 hours or overnight.

Heat the oil in a wok or large skillet. Add the onion, garlic and ginger and stir-fry over medium heat 2 to 3 minutes. Drain the marinade from the steak and reserve, add the meat to the wok and stir-fry over high heat 3 to 4 minutes. Add the remaining vegetables and stir-fry 2 to 3 minutes.

Add the marinade and cook, stirring, until bubbly and juices thicken slightly. Adjust seasoning to taste and serve immediately with cooked noodles or brown rice.

Makes 4 servings.

Each serving contains:				*Exchanges*:	
Calories	310	Total Fat	10g	Bread	0.4
Protein	37g	Saturated Fat	3g	Vegetable	1.4
Carbohydrates	14g	Cholesterol	78mg	Meat	4.0
Fiber	3g	Sodium	647mg	Fat	1.0

Beef Casserole with Beer

As it slowly cooks and becomes tender, chuck steak adds succulent flavor to long-simmered stews and casseroles.

A rich-tasting casserole that is perfect for winter evenings. Replace the beer with stock if you prefer.

1	tablespoon olive or sunflower oil
2	lb. lean beef chuck steak, trimmed and cubed
2	large onions, sliced
2	garlic cloves, crushed
2	large carrots, peeled and sliced
8	oz. button mushrooms, halved
1	tablespoon all-purpose flour
1-1/2	cups beef stock
1/2	cup beer or ale
1	bay leaf
1	teaspoon dried Italian seasoning
	Salt and freshly ground black pepper

Preheat oven to 350F (175C). Heat the oil in a Dutch oven or large ovenproof casserole dish over medium heat. Add beef, onions and garlic and cook, stirring occasionally, 10 minutes or until the beef is browned. Add the carrots and mushrooms and cook 5 minutes or until carrots are softened. Add the flour and stir well. Pour in the stock and beer and stir well. Add the bay leaf, herbs, salt and pepper. Bring to a boil. Cover and bake 2-1/2 hours or until the beef is tender. Stir occasionally during cooking. Remove bay leaf before serving. Serve with boiled potatoes and cooked vegetables.

Makes 4 to 6 servings.

For 4 servings, each serving contains:

				Exchanges:	
Calories	911	Total Fat	63g	Bread	0.2
Protein	66g	Saturated Fat	24g	Vegetable	2.0
Carbohydrates	16g	Cholesterol	225mg	Meat	7.9
Fiber	3g	Sodium	313mg	Fat	8.7

Ham-and-Pineapple Stir-fry

A colorful and delicious stir-fry. Use canned pineapple in natural juice rather than syrup to reduce the sugar content.

1	tablespoon olive or sunflower oil
6	oz. lean ham steak, trimmed and cut into thin strips
1/2	red bell pepper, seeded and sliced
1/2	green bell pepper, seeded and sliced
4	oz. baby sweet corn, sliced into small pieces
	Freshly ground black pepper
1	(8-oz.) can pineapple pieces in natural juice, drained and juice reserved
2	teaspoons cornstarch

Heat the oil in a skillet or wok over medium heat. Add the ham and cook, stirring, 1 to 2 minutes or until slightly browned. Add the bell peppers, corn and black pepper and stir-fry 2 to 3 minutes. Mix the cornstarch with a little of the reserved pineapple juice and add to the stir-fry with remaining juice and pineapple. Stir-fry over high heat 2 or 3 minutes or until the sauce has thickened. Serve immediately over rice.

Makes 2 servings.

Each serving (excluding rice) contains:

				Exchanges:	
Calories	277	Total Fat	11g	Bread	0.4
Protein	19g	Saturated Fat	2g	Vegetable	0.5
Carbohydrates	27g	Cholesterol	40mg	Fruit	1.1
Fiber	3g	Sodium	1226mg	Meat	2.0
				Fat	1.3

Chicken, Spicy Sausage and Seafood Paella

Fresh Mussels

When using fresh mussels, make sure that you discard any that remain open when tapped with your finger and any that do not open when they are cooked.

There are many different versions of this popular Spanish dish. If desired, substitute the same weight of firm white fish for the mussels. Traditionally, saffron is used to color and flavor this dish. Turmeric is less expensive but does not taste the same. Saffron is usually available in the spice section of the supermarket and you need only add a pinch in place of the turmeric for the authentic flavor.

  2 tablespoons olive or corn oil
  1 large onion, finely chopped
  2 garlic cloves, crushed
  1 red bell pepper, seeded and sliced
  1 green bell pepper, seeded and sliced
  1 lb. boneless, skinless chicken breasts, cut into
       1-inch pieces
  3 oz. chorizo sausage, sliced
  1 (8-oz.) can chopped tomatoes
  1 cup brown rice
     Generous pinch of saffron or 2 teaspoons turmeric
  2 cups chicken broth
  6 oz. peeled shrimp
  6 oz. mussels in shells, scrubbed
  2 tablespoons chopped fresh parsley

Heat the oil in a large wok or paella pan over medium heat. Add the onion, garlic, bell peppers and chicken and cook, stirring occasionally, 5 minutes or until vegetables are soft. Stir in the sausage, tomatoes, rice, saffron or turmeric and broth. Bring to a boil. Reduce heat, cover and simmer 15 minutes. Stir the paella and cook, uncovered, 15 minutes.

Add the shrimp, mussels and parsley, return to a boil, lower heat and simmer, uncovered, 5 to 10 minutes or until the mussels open, the liquid is absorbed and the rice is tender. Discard any mussels that do not open. Serve immediately with crusty bread and a crisp green salad.

Makes 4 to 6 servings.

For 4 servings, each serving contains:				*Exchanges*:	
Calories	593g	Total Fat	21g	Bread	2.1
Protein	52g	Saturated Fat	6g	Vegetable	1.5
Carbohydrates	46g	Cholesterol	181mg	Meat	5.0
Fiber	3g	Sodium	1020mg	Fat	2.5

Lamb Rhogan

This makes a rather hot curry. Adjust the amount of curry powder to suit your taste. Serve with cooked brown rice.

1	tablespoon olive or sunflower oil
1-1/4	lb. lean lamb cubes, fat removed
1	large onion, sliced
2	garlic cloves, crushed
1	tablespoon hot curry powder
1	teaspoon turmeric
1	cup chicken broth
1	(14-oz.) can chopped tomatoes
1	medium potato, peeled and diced
2	carrots, diced
2	tablespoons raisins

Heat the oil in a large saucepan, add the lamb, onion and garlic and cook, stirring occasionally, 5 minutes or until browned. Stir in the curry powder and turmeric and cook 1 minute, stirring constantly. Stir in the broth and tomatoes, cover and simmer 40 minutes, or until the lamb is tender. Stir in the potato, carrot and raisins.

Cover and simmer 15 minutes or until vegetables are almost tender. Cook, uncovered, 15 minutes or until sauce is slightly reduced.

Makes 4 servings.

A good curry should not be watery, so cook uncovered for the last 15 minutes until the sauce is well reduced and coats all the ingredients.

Indian Meal for Four

Cheese-and-Spinach Filo Triangles (page 36)

Lamb Rhogan (opposite) served with rice

Pears with Ginger Sauce (page 157)

Each serving contains:

				Exchanges:	
				Bread	0.4
Calories	450	Total Fat	17g	Vegetable	1.8
Protein	51g	Saturated Fat	5g	Fruit	0.3
Carbohydrates	22g	Cholesterol	153mg	Meat	5.7
Fiber	3g	Sodium	471mg	Fat	0.7

Spicy Hungarian Goulash

Goulash is traditionally a spicy dish, but you can vary the amount and type of paprika according to your taste. My husband and I both like spicy food, so I use hot paprika.

1	tablespoon olive or sunflower oil
2	lb. lean beef round steak, fat removed, cubed
2	onions, thinly sliced
1 to 2	tablespoons hot or mild paprika
1	tablespoon all-purpose flour
1	tablespoon chopped fresh marjoram or dill weed
2	cups beef stock
	Salt and freshly ground black pepper
3	tablespoons sour cream

Heat the oil in a large heavy saucepan. Add the beef and onions and cook, stirring occasionally, 4 to 5 minutes or until brown. Stir in the paprika, flour and marjoram and cook, stirring, 2 minutes. Gradually stir in the stock, salt and pepper. Bring to a boil, reduce the heat, cover and simmer 1-1/2 hours or until the beef is tender.

Spoon into warmed bowls and top with the sour cream. Sprinkle with a little paprika and serve with fresh crusty bread.

Makes 4 servings.

Each serving contains:

				Exchanges:	
Calories	497	Total Fat	19g	Bread	0.1
Protein	69g	Saturated Fat	7g	Vegetable	0.7
Carbohydrates	7g	Cholesterol	161mg	Meat	7.9
Fiber	1g	Sodium	317mg	Fat	1.1

Make-ahead Lasagna

When our daughter Jade was a baby, I found lasagna was the easiest dish to make for dinner when we had company. I could prepare it well before they arrived so that I had more time with our guests and Jade.

This dish can be frozen— freeze after adding the cheese sauce and before baking. Thaw completely in the refrigerator and then bake as in the recipe. Serve with salad and crusty bread.

2	medium onions, finely chopped
1	garlic clove
1-1/2	lb. lean ground beef
8	oz. mushrooms, sliced
1	teaspoon dried oregano
1	teaspoon dried basil
2	tablespoons tomato paste
2	(14-oz.) cans chopped tomatoes
1/2	cup beef stock
	Salt and freshly ground black pepper
2	tablespoons vegetable-oil spread
2	tablespoons all-purpose flour
1-1/2	cups nonfat milk
4	oz. (about 1 cup) shredded reduced-fat Cheddar cheese
8	or 9 sheets green lasagna noodles, cooked

Cook the onions, garlic, beef and mushrooms in a large nonstick pan over medium heat, stirring to break up meat, 5 minutes or until the meat is browned. Drain off any excess fat. Add the herbs, tomato paste, tomatoes, stock, salt and pepper. Bring to a boil, stirring occasionally. Half cover and simmer, stirring occasionally, 30 minutes or until the sauce is thickened and well reduced.

Preheat oven to 375F (190C). Meanwhile, make the cheese sauce. Melt the vegetable spread in a saucepan over medium heat. Stir in the flour and cook 1 minute. Stir in the milk, bring to a boil and cook, stirring, 1 to 2 minutes or until thickened. Remove from the heat and stir in 1/4 cup of the cheese. Season with salt and pepper.

Place half the meat sauce in the bottom of a large baking dish. Cover with a layer of noodles. Repeat with the remaining meat sauce, finishing with a layer of noodles. Pour the cheese sauce over the noodles and sprinkle with the remaining cheese.

Bake 40 minutes or until golden brown and bubbly. Let stand 10 minutes before serving.

Makes 6 servings.

Each serving contains:				*Exchanges:*	
				Bread	1.6
Calories	572	Total Fat	24g	Vegetable	2.0
Protein	46g	Saturated Fat	9g	Milk	0.2
Carbohydrates	40g	Cholesterol	117mg	Meat	4.6
Fiber	4g	Sodium	521mg	Fat	2.1

Pork-and-Apricot Casserole

Pinto beans are an important ingredient in Mexican cooking. They have a pale pink skin and small brown blotches or speckles, hence the name pinto, *which means "painted" in Spanish.*

This recipe uses beans and apricots to replace some of the meat. They add a richness to the sauce and make the meal more filling.

1	tablespoon olive or corn oil
1	lb. lean pork tenderloin, cubed
1	large onion, finely chopped
1	medium green bell pepper, seeded and sliced
1	medium red bell pepper, seeded and sliced
1	tablespoon all-purpose flour
1	(15-oz.) can pinto beans, drained
1	teaspoon ground turmeric
	Salt and freshly ground black pepper
2	cups chicken broth
3	oz. (about 1/2 cup) dried apricots, chopped
1	tablespoon lemon juice

Preheat oven to 350F (175C). Heat the oil in a Dutch oven or ovenproof casserole dish over medium heat. Add the pork and onion and cook, stirring frequently, 5 minutes or until the pork is browned. Add the bell peppers and cook 2 minutes. Stir in the flour, beans, turmeric, salt and pepper. Gradually stir in the broth. Bring to a boil. Cover and bake 1 hour. Stir in the apricots and lemon juice. Add a little more stock if casserole is too dry. Bake 15 minutes. Serve immediately with potatoes and cooked green vegetables.

Makes 4 servings.

Each serving contains:

				Exchanges:	
				Bread	1.4
Calories	489	Total Fat	12g	Vegetable	1.0
Protein	47g	Saturated Fat	3g	Fruit	0.9
Carbohydrates	48g	Cholesterol	107mg	Meat	4.6
Fiber	12g	Sodium	601mg	Fat	0.7

Chicken Bake

This dish is useful to serve when you have leftover cooked chicken. Vary the vegetables to suit your own taste. For example, use peas instead of corn, or carrots in place of the broccoli.

3	tablespoons soft margarine
1	medium onion, finely chopped
2	tablespoons all-purpose flour
1-1/2	cups nonfat milk
1	(10-oz.) pkg. frozen broccoli spears, thawed and drained
3/4	cup cooked or canned whole-kernel corn
8	oz. cooked chicken, diced
	Salt and freshly ground black pepper
2	oz. (about 1/2 cup) shredded reduced-fat Cheddar cheese

Preheat oven to 350F (175C). Lightly grease a 2-quart casserole dish. Melt the margarine in a medium saucepan over low heat. Add the onion and cook 5 minutes or until soft. Stir in the flour and cook, stirring, 1 minute. Gradually blend in the milk and bring to a boil, stirring constantly. Cook, stirring, 1 to 2 minutes or until thick. Stir in the broccoli, corn and cooked chicken, and season with salt.

Turn the mixture into the prepared dish. Bake 25 minutes or until bubbly. Sprinkle with the cheese and bake until cheese melts. Serve hot with new potatoes and a green salad.

Makes 4 servings.

Each serving contains:

				Exchanges:	
Calories	314	Total Fat	15g	Bread	0.5
Protein	27g	Saturated Fat	3g	Vegetable	1.1
Carbohydrates	20g	Cholesterol	52mg	Milk	0.4
Fiber	3g	Sodium	420mg	Meat	2.5
				Fat	1.7

Rock Cornish Hen with Walnuts

Rock Cornish hens are usually served one per person. They are available in the frozen-food section in the supermarket.

Unlike regular chickens, Cornish hens have all dark meat.

1	tablespoon olive or sunflower oil
4	Rock Cornish hens, thawed and rinsed
2	shallots, peeled and chopped
1	tablespoon cornstarch
2	tablespoons cold water
2	cups chicken broth
1/2	cup dry white wine
1/2	cup walnut halves, toasted
	Salt and freshly ground black pepper
2	tablespoons chopped fresh parsley

Preheat oven to 325F (165C). Heat the oil in a large Dutch oven over medium heat. Add the hens and shallots. Cook, turning often, until browned. Mix the cornstarch with the water and stir into the Dutch oven with the broth and wine. Stir in the walnuts, salt and pepper. Bring to a boil. Cover and bake 1-1/2 hours or until the hens are tender. Stir in the parsley and adjust seasoning if necessary. Serve with wild rice and green vegetables.

Makes 4 servings.

Each serving contains:

Calories	891	Total Fat	53g	Bread	0.3
Protein	88g	Saturated Fat	13g	Vegetable	0.3
Carbohydrates	6g	Cholesterol	268mg	Meat	12.2
Fiber	1g	Sodium	1482mg	Fat	2.0

Exchanges:

Bolognese Sauce

Spaghetti Bolognese is a family favorite. Adding extra vegetables, such as carrots and mushrooms, makes the meat go further and I think adds extra interest to this recipe.

1	lb. lean ground beef
1	medium onion, finely chopped
1	garlic clove, crushed
2	large carrots, finely diced
8	oz. mushrooms, sliced
1	(14-oz.) can chopped tomatoes
2	tablespoons tomato paste
2	cups beef stock
1/2	teaspoon dried oregano
1/2	teaspoon dried basil
	Salt and freshly ground black pepper

Place the ground beef, onion and garlic in a large nonstick pan over medium heat. Cook until browned, stirring to break up beef. Drain off any excess fat. Add the remaining ingredients and season with salt and pepper. Stir well. Bring to a boil. Reduce heat, cover and simmer 40 minutes, stirring occasionally. Serve over freshly cooked spaghetti.

Makes 4 or 5 servings.

Each serving (not including spaghetti) contains: *Exchanges:*

Calories	387	Total Fat	19g	Vegetable	2.3
Protein	38g	Saturated Fat	7g	Fruit	0.1
Carbohydrates	15g	Cholesterol	112mg	Meat	4.0
Fiber	3g	Sodium	504mg	Fat	1.4

Thirty-minute Macaroni

Two sauces—a beef-tomato sauce on the bottom and a cheese sauce over the pasta—make this a taste treat.

Suitable for freezing. After adding the sauce and shredded cheese, cool and freeze. Thaw in the refrigerator and then bake at 350F (175C) 20 to 25 minutes until piping hot and golden brown.

1	lb. lean ground beef
1	large onion, chopped
2	large carrots, diced
1	tablespoon dried mixed herbs
2	tablespoons tomato paste
1	cup beef stock
1	(14-oz.) can chopped tomatoes
1	(7-oz.) can whole-kernel corn
	Salt and freshly ground black pepper
7	oz. macaroni or penne
1/4	cup soft margarine
1/4	cup all-purpose flour
1	cup 2% lowfat milk
4	oz. (about 1 cup) shredded reduced-fat Cheddar cheese

Place the beef, onion and carrots in a large nonstick pan over medium heat. Cook 5 minutes, stirring to break up beef, or until the beef is browned. Drain off any excess fat. Return to the heat and stir in the herbs, tomato paste, stock and tomatoes. Bring to a boil, cover and simmer 15 minutes. Add the corn and cook 5 minutes. Season with salt and pepper.

Meanwhile, boil the pasta in lightly salted boiling water according to the package instructions until tender.

Combine the margarine, flour and and some milk in a saucepan. Whisk in remaining milk and cook over medium heat, stirring constantly, until the sauce thickens. Stir in 3/4 of the cheese until melted. Season with salt and pepper.

Pour the beef mixture into an ovenproof dish. Drain the pasta and arrange over the beef mixture. Spoon the cheese sauce over the pasta to cover. Sprinkle with the remaining cheese. Broil about 10 minutes or until golden brown and heated through. Serve hot with a green salad or freshly cooked vegetables.

Makes 4 to 5 servings.

Each serving contains:

Calories	817	Total Fat	35g
Protein	54g	Saturated Fat	12g
Carbohydrates	72g	Cholesterol	123mg
Fiber	6g	Sodium	787mg

Exchanges:

Bread	3.5
Vegetable	2.3
Fruit	0.1
Milk	0.2
Meat	4.9
Fat	3.9

Marinated Chicken and Rosemary Kebabs

A rosemary-enhanced dish that is ideal for barbecues. Serve with Greek Salad (page 57) and cooked brown rice or couscous.

1-1/2	lb. boneless, skinless chicken breasts, trimmed and cut into 2-inch pieces
3	tablespoons olive oil
3	tablespoons lemon juice
2	tablespoons fresh rosemary leaves
	Freshly ground black pepper

Thread the chicken onto metal skewers and lay in a shallow dish. Mix the oil, lemon juice, rosemary and pepper together in a small bowl and pour the marinade over the kebabs. Cover and refrigerate 2 hours.

Preheat broiler. Arrange kebabs in a baking pan. Broil kebabs about 10 to 15 minutes or until the chicken is cooked through, brushing with the marinade during the first 5 minutes. Turn frequently. Serve hot.

Makes 4 servings.

Each serving contains:

				Exchanges:	
Calories	272	Total Fat	14g	Meat	3.2
Protein	34g	Saturated Fat	2g	Fat	2.0
Carbohydrates	0g	Cholesterol	94mg		
Fiber	0g	Sodium	82mg		

Chicken in Wine Sauce

Savor the traditional French *coq au vin*.

2	tablespoons olive oil
4	boneless, skinless chicken breasts
12	boiling onions, peeled
2	garlic cloves, crushed
2	slices lean bacon, chopped
5	oz. button mushrooms, halved
1	tablespoon all-purpose flour
1-1/2	cups chicken broth
1	cup dry red Burgundy wine
1	bouquet garni
	Salt and freshly ground black pepper
2	tablespoons chopped fresh parsley to garnish

Don't be put off by the large amount of wine used, because most of the alcohol evaporates during cooking.

This dish can be frozen up to 3 months. Thaw thoroughly in the refrigerator before reheating in the oven until piping hot. Serve with crusty bread or boiled potatoes and fresh vegetables.

Preheat oven to 350F (175C). Heat the oil in a large pan over medium heat. Add the chicken and cook until browned, turning occasionally. Drain and transfer the chicken to a large casserole dish.

Add the onions, garlic and bacon to the pan and cook until golden. Spoon into the casserole dish. Add the mushrooms and cook 2 to 3 minutes. Stir in the flour and cook 1 minute, stirring. Gradually add the chicken broth, wine, bouquet garni, salt and pepper. Bring to a boil, then pour over the chicken pieces. Cover and bake 1 hour or until the chicken and onions are tender. Remove the bouquet garni and sprinkle with chopped parsley.

Makes 4 servings.

Each serving contains:

				Exchanges:	
Calories	323	Total Fat	12g	Bread	0.1
Protein	31g	Saturated Fat	3g	Vegetable	1.7
Carbohydrates	12g	Cholesterol	76mg	Fruit	0.1
Fiber	1g	Sodium	550mg	Meat	2.6
				Fat	2.4

Georgia Chicken

Peanuts add an unexpected crunch to the sauce and make it a little bit different.

Cajun seasoning is a hot, spicy mixture redolent of the Deep South. It usually contains salt, so you won't need to add any more salt to the dish, but it also contains a powerful blend of herbs and spices. These may include chili powder, black pepper, garlic, allspice, coriander seed, cumin, fennel seed, cardamom, mustard, thyme, sage and oregano.

4	boneless, skinless chicken breasts
3	tablespoons soft margarine, melted
1	teaspoon Cajun seasoning
2	medium onions, coarsely chopped
2	tablespoons all-purpose flour
2	cups nonfat milk
1/4	teaspoon each dried thyme and oregano
1	(8-oz.) can whole-kernel corn, drained
1/4	cup unsalted dry-roasted peanuts
	Pinch of cayenne pepper

Preheat oven to 350F (175C). Brush the chicken with a little of the melted margarine and sprinkle with the Cajun seasoning. Place in a baking pan and bake about 30 minutes, turning halfway through cooking, or until chicken is white in center when cut with a knife.

About 15 minutes before the end of cooking time, heat the remaining margarine in a saucepan over medium heat. Add the onions and cook, stirring occasionally, until softened, 3 to 4 minutes. Stir in the flour and gradually blend in the milk. Bring to a boil, stirring constantly. Add the herbs and stir in the corn. Transfer the chicken to a serving dish, pour the sauce over the chicken and sprinkle with the peanuts and cayenne pepper. Serve hot with brown rice and cooked broccoli.

Makes 4 servings.

Each serving contains:

				Exchanges:	
Calories	395	Total Fat	17g	Bread	0.9
Protein	36g	Saturated Fat	3g	Vegetable	0.7
Carbohydrates	26g	Cholesterol	75mg	Fruit	0.1
Fiber	3g	Sodium	391mg	Milk	0.5
				Meat	2.8
				Fat	2.4

Chicken Marengo

Because little oil is used to brown the chicken, you may need to stir or turn the meat more frequently to prevent it from sticking.

Marengo *means the dish is cooked in a sauce of mushrooms, tomatoes and garlic. It is said to have come from a dish that was cooked for Napoleon immediately after the battle of Marengo on June 14, 1800, from the only ingredients that were available.*

1	tablespoon all-purpose flour
	Salt and freshly ground black pepper
4	boneless, skinless chicken breasts
2	tablespoons olive or sunflower oil
1	large onion, sliced
2	garlic cloves, crushed
4	oz. button mushrooms, wiped
2	(14-oz.) cans chopped tomatoes
1/2	cup chicken broth
2	tablespoons brandy

Season the flour with salt and pepper. Coat the chicken breasts with the flour. Heat the oil in a large skillet or Dutch oven over medium heat. Add the chicken and cook, turning, 5 to 10 minutes or until golden brown. Remove with a slotted spoon and reserve. Add the onion, garlic and mushrooms to the skillet and cook 5 minutes, or until soft. Return the chicken to the skillet with the remaining ingredients. Season with salt and pepper. Bring to a boil. Reduce heat, cover and simmer 1 hour or until the chicken is tender.

Transfer the chicken to a warmed serving dish. If the sauce is too thin, boil briskly to reduce slightly and thicken. Spoon the sauce over the chicken and serve hot with cooked brown rice or pasta.

Makes 4 servings.

Each serving contains:

				Exchanges:	
Calories	291	Total Fat	11g	Bread	0.1
Protein	30g	Saturated Fat	2g	Vegetable	2.4
Carbohydrates	15g	Cholesterol	73mg	Meat	2.5
Fiber	3g	Sodium	620mg	Fat	1.6

Chicken Tikka

This comes from an authentic recipe from my brother's friend Mohammed. Serve with a side salad and steamed rice. If you use wooden skewers, soak them in water before threading on the meat. This keeps them from burning during cooking.

2/3	cup fat-free plain yogurt
1	tablespoon ground ginger
1	tablespoon chili powder
1	tablespoon ground coriander
2	teaspoon olive or sunflower oil
2	garlic cloves, crushed
	Salt
1	teaspoon lemon juice
4	boneless, skinless chicken breasts, cubed

Stir together the yogurt, spices, oil, garlic, salt and lemon juice in a large bowl. Stir in the chicken. Cover and marinate in the refrigerator overnight.

Preheat broiler. Remove chicken from marinade. Thread the chicken on skewers and place in a baking pan. Grill 8 to 10 minutes, until cooked through, basting with the marinade during the first 5 minutes of cooking only.

Makes 4 servings.

Tikka is a Hindi word that roughly translated means "kebab."

These skewered sticks of meat would also be ideal to cook on a grill.

Each serving contains:

Calories	184	Total Fat	5g	Milk	0.3
Protein	29g	Saturated Fat	1g	Meat	2.5
Carbohydrates	3g	Cholesterol	74mg	Fat	0.4
Fiber	0g	Sodium	228mg		

Exchanges:

Cowboy's Supper

This quick-and-easy family supper is convenient to make because it is cooked quickly on the stove top. Sausages and beans are a traditional combination that is popular with children. Serve with mashed potato for a campfire-style supper.

It is much easier to persuade children to eat what is good for them if it looks like fun. Serve this in true western style on enamel camping plates.

1	lb. reduced-fat precooked chicken or turkey sausages
1	tablespoon olive or corn oil
1	large onion, sliced
2	large carrots, diced
1	(14-oz.) can chopped tomatoes
1	tablespoon dried mixed herbs
1	(8-oz.) can pork and beans
1/2	cup vegetable or chicken stock
	Salt and freshly ground black pepper

Cut the sausages into bite-size pieces and set aside. Heat the oil in a large saucepan over medium heat. Add the onion and carrots and cook 5 minutes, stirring occasionally. Stir in the sausages and the remaining ingredients. Bring to a boil. Reduce heat, cover and simmer 20 to 25 minutes or until the sauce has thickened slightly and the vegetables are tender.

Makes 4 or 5 servings.

For 4 servings, each serving contains:

				Exchanges:	
Calories	403	Total Fat	23g	Bread	0.5
Protein	29g	Saturated Fat	7g	Vegetable	1.8
Carbohydrates	23g	Cholesterol	96mg	Fruit	0.2
Fiber	6g	Sodium	1308mg	Meat	4.2
				Fat	0.7

Pasta

Pasta dishes are satisfying and economical, as well as a good source of complex carbohydrates. Pasta combines with an unlimited variety of meats, vegetables, fish and nuts. Try experimenting with different shapes and varieties. Some pastas are available in whole-wheat, which are higher in fiber, but any type is suitable for healthful eating, providing it is not smothered in high-fat sauces.

Spaghetti Tossed with Turkey and Walnuts

Crunchy nuts and tender turkey combine to give a totally different texture and flavor to this pasta dish. If you have a carbohydrate allowance per meal, you can vary the amount of spaghetti to suit your needs—2 ounces of dry pasta provide approximately 35 grams of carbohydrate.

Serve with a crisp green salad and finish with fresh fruit for a delicious meal in minutes.

9   oz. whole-wheat spaghetti, cooked
2   oz. olive or sunflower oil
10   oz. turkey ham, chopped
1   garlic clove, crushed
2   oz. walnuts, chopped
1   (14-oz.) can chopped tomatoes
2   tablespoons freshly chopped parsley
     Freshly ground black pepper

Drain the spaghetti and place in a serving bowl.

Heat the oil in a medium saucepan over medium heat. Add the turkey ham, garlic and walnuts and cook until golden, stirring constantly. Stir in the tomatoes and parsley and heat, stirring constantly, 2 to 3 minutes or until piping hot. Season with black pepper. Add sauce to spaghetti and toss to combine. Serve hot.

Makes 4 servings.

Each serving contains:

Calories	438	Total Fat	19g	Bread	2.4
Protein	24g	Saturated Fat	3g	Vegetable	0.9
Carbohydrates	47g	Cholesterol	52mg	Meat	0.8
Fiber	7g	Sodium	937mg	Fat	3.1

Exchanges:

Spinach-and-Cheese Macaroni

Pasta dishes such as this can provide the ideal ratio of fat, carbohydrate and protein for healthful eating. This recipe has around 55% of calories from carbohydrate, 20% from fat and 20% from protein.

This colorful dish adds a new dimension to baked macaroni.

10	oz. macaroni, preferably whole-wheat
2	tablespoons soft margarine
2	tablespoons all-purpose flour
1-1/2	cups nonfat milk
	Freshly ground black pepper
4	oz. (about 1/2 cup) shredded reduced-fat Cheddar cheese
1	(10-oz.) pkg. frozen chopped spinach, thawed

Preheat oven to 350F (175C). Lightly grease a large casserole dish. Cook the macaroni in boiling water according to the package instructions until tender and drain well.

Meanwhile, melt the margarine in a saucepan. Stir in the flour and cook 1 minute. Stir in the milk, bring to a boil and cook, stirring, 1 to 2 minutes or until thickened. Remove from the heat and season with pepper. Stir in half the cheese and all of the cooked macaroni. Drain the spinach and cook in a small saucepan 3 minutes. Drain well and stir into the macaroni mixture. Turn into greased dish and sprinkle with the remaining cheese.

Bake 20 minutes or until the cheese topping is bubbling and golden brown.

Makes 4 servings.

Each serving contains:

				Exchanges:	
Calories	367	Total Fat	9g	Bread	2.7
Protein	21g	Saturated Fat	3g	Vegetable	0.5
Carbohydrates	55g	Cholesterol	8mg	Milk	0.4
Fiber	7g	Sodium	148mg	Meat	0.9
				Fat	1.5

Mushroom-and-Chicken Tagliatelle

This is comfort food at its best!

Mushrooms are tasty as well as a useful ingredient in a healthful diet. They add bulk to the dish and they are delicious and meaty in their own right. They are low in salt, have no cholesterol, carbohydrates or fat but are a good source of vegetable protein as well as important B-group vitamins and potassium.

12	oz. tagliatelle
1	tablespoon olive or corn oil
1	small onion, finely chopped
1	garlic clove, crushed
8	oz. brown mushrooms, sliced
1	boneless, skinless chicken breast, cooked and coarsely chopped
2	tablespoons cornstarch
2	tablespoons cold water
1-1/2	cups chicken broth
1/2	cup 2% lowfat milk
	Salt and freshly ground black pepper

Cook the tagliatelle in boiling water according to the package instructions until tender, and drain.

Meanwhile, heat the oil in a nonstick skillet or wok over medium heat. Add the onion, garlic and mushrooms and cook 3 to 4 minutes until softened. Stir in the chicken and cook 1 to 2 minutes or until browned. Mix the cornstarch with the water and add to the pan, stirring constantly. Gradually stir in the broth and milk. Season to taste and stir until thickened. Serve spooned over the tagliatelle.

Makes 4 servings.

Each serving contains:

				Exchanges:	
				Bread	3.8
Calories	407	Total Fat	7g	Vegetable	0.8
Protein	20g	Saturated Fat	1g	Milk	0.1
Carbohydrates	65g	Cholesterol	21mg	Meat	0.6
Fiber	4g	Sodium	459mg	Fat	0.8

Stir-fried Shredded Pork and Pasta

I've called for 8 ounces of pasta, which yields 35 grams carbohydrate per serving. Vary the amount of pasta to suit your appetite.

Add vegetables to the stir-fry if desired, such as green or red bell peppers or baby corn.

1	lb. lean pork, diced and trimmed of fat
4	tablespoons white-wine vinegar
2	tablespoons soy sauce
2	tablespoons tomato paste
8	oz. dried whole-wheat pasta
1	tablespoon olive or corn oil
2	teaspoons cornstarch
2	tablespoons water
1	(8-oz.) can pineapple pieces in natural juice

Place the pork in a bowl and mix with the vinegar, soy sauce and tomato paste. Cover and marinate in the refrigerator 2 hours. Cook the pasta in boiling water according to the package instructions.

Drain the marinade mixture and reserve. Heat the oil in a nonstick skillet or wok over medium heat. Add the pork and stir-fry 4 to 5 minutes. Add the reserved marinade. Mix the cornstarch with the water and add to the pan with the pineapple pieces and juice. Bring to a boil, stirring constantly, until the sauce thickens.

Drain the pasta and return to the hot pan. Stir in the pork and sauce. Toss together and serve.

Makes 4 servings.

Each serving contains:

				Exchanges:	
Calories	463	Total Fat	11g	Bread	2.1
Protein	43g	Saturated Fat	3g	Vegetable	0.1
Carbohydrates	49g	Cholesterol	107mg	Fruit	0.6
Fiber	6g	Sodium	546mg	Meat	4.5
				Fat	1.6

Ham-and-Tomato Pasta Sauce

This could also be served as a delicious filling for a baked potato but if you have a carbohydrate allowance for each meal, be sure to add the carbohydrate values for the potato or pasta that you serve with this sauce.

Two ounces of dry pasta provide approximately 35 grams of carbohydrate. A 7-ounce potato provides approximately 40 grams of carbohydrate.

As a variation, use thin strips of cooked pork or chicken in place of the ham.

2   teaspoons olive or sunflower oil
1   onion, finely chopped
1   garlic clove, crushed
1   (14-oz.) can chopped tomatoes
1   tablespoon tomato paste
3   tablespoons chopped fresh parsley
4   oz. ham, cut into cubes

Heat the oil in a saucepan over medium heat. Add the onion and garlic and cook 5 minutes or until soft, stirring occasionally. Stir in the tomatoes, tomato paste and chopped parsley. Cover and simmer 5 minutes or until the sauce has thickened. Add the ham and simmer another 5 minutes. Serve over cooked whole-wheat pasta.

Makes 2 servings.

Each serving contains:

Calories	182	Total Fat	8g	Vegetable	2.4
Protein	14g	Saturated Fat	2g	Fruit	0.1
Carbohydrates	15g	Cholesterol	27mg	Meat	1.4
Fiber	3g	Sodium	1200mg	Fat	0.9

Exchanges:

Chicken-Sausage Sauce

Choose reduced-fat sausage and drain well after cooking to reduce the fat in the finished recipe.

2	tablespoons olive oil
1	large onion, finely chopped
8	oz. boneless, skinless chicken breast, chopped
4	oz. bulk spicy pork sausage
1	cup canned crushed tomatoes in purée
1/2	cup chicken broth
	Salt and freshly ground black pepper
3	tablespoons freshly chopped parsley

Heat the oil in a nonstick skillet with lid over medium heat. Add the onion and cook 3 to 4 minutes. Add chicken and sausage and cook, stirring to break up sausage, until sausage is browned. Drain off fat.

Stir in the tomatoes and broth and bring to a boil. Cover and simmer 10 to 15 minutes, stirring occasionally. Season with salt and pepper and stir in the chopped parsley. Serve with freshly cooked pasta.

Makes 4 servings.

Each serving contains:

				Exchanges:	
Calories	270	Total Fat	17g	Vegetable	1.5
Protein	19g	Saturated Fat	4g	Meat	1.8
Carbohydrates	10g	Cholesterol	55mg	Fat	2.6
Fiber	2g	Sodium	875mg		

Ten-minute Carbonara

Friends often tell me they like recipes that can be prepared quickly when they get home from work. Well, this recipe is ideal because it takes very little preparation. Serve with a crisp salad and fresh crusty bread if desired.

10	oz. whole-wheat spaghetti
4	oz. mushrooms, sliced
1/2	cup whole-milk cream
1	egg, beaten
1	oz. (about 1/4 cup) shredded reduced-fat Cheddar cheese
2	tablespoons chopped fresh parsley
6	oz. lean ham, cut into thin strips
8	oz. cooked lean chicken, cut into strips
	Salt and freshly ground black pepper

Cook the spaghetti in a large pan in boiling water just until tender. Add the mushrooms to the spaghetti 2 minutes before the end of cooking time. Beat the milk, egg, cheese and parsley together. Drain the spaghetti and return to the hot pan. Stir in the ham, chicken, milk mixture, salt and pepper. Toss together over medium heat until hot. Serve immediately.

Makes 4 servings.

Each serving contains:

Calories	468	Total Fat	14g	Bread	2.5
Protein	39g	Saturated Fat	7g	Vegetable	0.3
Carbohydrates	47g	Cholesterol	149mg	Meat	3.1
Fiber	7g	Sodium	814mg	Fat	1.6

Exchanges:

Red Pesto Pasta

Pesto sauce may be purchased in jars, but it is easy to make at home and you benefit from the delicious aroma and taste of fresh basil.

If you don't grow your own basil, look for fresh basil leaves in the produce section of the supermarket.

1/2	oz. fresh basil leaves, chopped
1	garlic clove, crushed
2	tablespoons pine nuts
2	oz. (about 1/3 cup) freshly grated Parmesan cheese
1	(11-oz.) jar sun-dried tomatoes in olive oil
14	oz. whole-wheat pasta
24	ripe olives, pitted

Place the basil, garlic and pine nuts in a food processor or blender. Process a few seconds. Add the cheese and process a few more seconds. Add half the tomatoes, with all of the olive oil, and blend a few seconds more to form a smooth paste.

Cook the pasta in boiling water just until tender, according to the package instructions. Drain and toss with the pesto sauce, olives and remaining tomatoes. Serve immediately with a green salad.

Makes 6 servings.

Each serving contains:

				Exchanges:	
Calories	476	Total Fat	24g	Bread	2.3
Protein	17g	Saturated Fat	5g	Vegetable	2.4
Carbohydrates	56g	Cholesterol	7mg	Meat	0.6
Fiber	10g	Sodium	473mg	Fat	2.7

Breads

Few things in life are more enticing than the aroma of freshly baked breads. This collection of recipes includes favorite quick breads made with fruit and whole-grain yeast breads. Most breads freeze well. Cool after baking, slice, wrap well and freeze up to three months. Although breads are high in carbohydrates, they can be an important part of a diabetic diet, particularly breads that are high in fiber.

Banana Bread

Dates add bulk to the mixture and replace the sugar and fat usually required in a cake recipe.

Best eaten within 2 days. Suitable for freezing.

An excellent way to use up bananas when they are too soft to enjoy raw.

Why not try replacing the sugar in some of your own recipes with a date purée? Dates contain around half the carbohydrate and calories as the same weight of sugar.

6	oz. pitted dried dates
1/2	cup water
1	egg
1	cup mashed ripe bananas (about 2 large)
1-3/4	cups all-purpose flour
1	teaspoon baking powder
1/4	teaspoon salt
1/4	teaspoon baking soda
1	teaspoon ground cinnamon
1/4	cup chopped walnuts

Preheat oven to 350F (175C). Grease a 9 x 5-inch loaf pan and line with waxed paper. Place the dates and water in a saucepan and simmer about 5 minutes or until the dates are soft. Mash with a fork until the dates are puréed. Allow to cool slightly. Beat in the egg and bananas. Mix together the flour, baking powder, salt, soda and cinnamon in a medium bowl. Stir the date mixture into the flour mixture just until flour is moistened. Stir in the walnuts.

Spoon the mixture into the prepared pan and smooth the surface. Bake 1 hour or until a skewer inserted in the center comes out clean. Cover with foil if becoming too brown. Allow to cool in the pan 15 minutes before turning out on a wire rack to cool completely. Cut into 14 slices.

Makes 1 loaf.

Each serving contains:

Calories	124	Total Fat	2g	Bread	0.7
Protein	3g	Saturated Fat	0g	Fruit	0.8
Carbohydrates	25g	Cholesterol	15mg	Meat	0.1
Fiber	2g	Sodium	92mg		

Exchanges:

Baking-powder Biscuits

Serve these hot for breakfast or to accompany a light lunch or supper.

2	cups all-purpose flour
4	teaspoons baking powder
1/2	teaspoon salt
2-1/2	tablespoons soft margarine
3/4	cup nonfat milk

Preheat oven to 450F (230C). Combine flour, baking powder and salt in a medium bowl. Cut in margarine until mixture resembles coarse cornmeal. Stir in milk to make a soft dough. Turn out dough on a lightly floured board. Knead lightly and roll out to 1/2-inch thickness. Cut into rounds with a 1-1/2-inch cutter. Arrange on a baking sheet. Bake 10 to 12 minutes or until puffed and golden brown.

Makes 24 (1-1/2-inch) biscuits.

Each biscuit contains:

Calories	52	Total Fat	1g
Protein	1g	Saturated Fat	0g
Carbohydrates	9g	Cholesterol	0mg
Fiber	0g	Sodium	120mg

Exchanges:

Bread	0.5
Fat	0.2

Raisin-Nut Muffins

Muffins are usually very high in calories. However, by cutting down on the sugar and fat content and increasing the fiber by using whole-wheat flour, these muffins are both nutritious and tasty.

For a substantial start to your day, serve with fresh fruit, tea or coffee and the newspaper.

1-1/3	cups whole-wheat flour
1	cup all-purpose flour
1/2	teaspoon salt
2	tablespoons baking powder
2	tablespoons sugar
1/4	cup soft margarine, melted
2	eggs, lightly beaten
1-1/4	cups nonfat milk
2	teaspoons vanilla extract
1/2	cup raisins
1/4	cup slivered almonds

Preheat oven to 400F (205C). Line a muffin pan with 12 paper cups. Sift the flours, salt and baking powder into a large bowl, adding any bran remaining in the sifter back into the bowl. In another bowl, mix together the sugar, margarine, eggs, milk and vanilla. Stir into the flour mixture until flour is moistened. Stir in raisins and almonds.

Spoon the mixture evenly into the paper cups, filling about 2/3 full. Bake 25 minutes or until golden. Serve warm or cool slightly before serving.

Makes 12 muffins.

Exchanges:

Each muffin contains:

				Exchanges	
				Bread	1.0
Calories	186	Total Fat	7g	Fruit	0.5
Protein	6g	Saturated Fat	1g	Milk	0.1
Carbohydrates	28g	Cholesterol	36mg	Meat	0.2
Fiber	2g	Sodium	331mg	Fat	1.1

Apricot-Pecan Slices

This delightful quick bread may also be served as a dessert.

Best eaten within 1 to 2 days. Suitable for freezing.

1-1/3   cups whole-wheat flour
1-1/3   cups all-purpose flour
1   tablespoon baking powder
2   teaspoons cinnamon
1/2   cup sugar
1/2   cup soft margarine, melted
2   eggs, lightly beaten
1/2   cup nonfat milk
1   (14-oz.) can apricots in juice, drained and chopped
1/2   cup pecans, chopped
Grated peel of 1 orange

Preheat oven to 350F (175C). Lightly grease an 11 x 7-inch baking pan and line bottom with waxed paper. Sift together the flours, baking powder and cinnamon into a large bowl, adding any bran remaining in the sifter back into the bowl. Stir in the sugar. Add the melted margarine, eggs and milk and stir until flour is moistened. Fold in the chopped apricots, nuts and grated orange peel. Pour into prepared pan. Bake 40 minutes or until golden and a skewer inserted in center comes out clean. Cool in the pan and cut into 16 slices.

Makes 16 slices.

Each slice contains:

					Exchanges:	
Calories	196	Total Fat	9g	Bread	0.9
Protein	4g	Saturated Fat	1g	Fruit	0.6
Carbohydrates	26g	Cholesterol	27mg	Meat	0.2
Fiber	2g	Sodium	134mg	Fat	1.6

Lemon-Sesame Bread

The lemon peel and juice add a lemony flavor to this bread accented with sesame seeds. It is best eaten within 2 to 3 days.

1/2	cup soft margarine
1/4	cup sugar
2	eggs, lightly beaten
1-1/4	cups all-purpose flour
1/2	cup whole-wheat flour
1	teaspoon baking powder
1	teaspoon baking soda
2/3	cup fat-free plain yogurt
2	tablespoons sesame seeds
	Grated peel and juice of 1 large lemon

Preheat oven to 325F (165C). Grease a 9 x 5-inch loaf pan and line with waxed paper. Cream the margarine and sugar together, then gradually beat in the eggs. Sift the flours, baking powder and soda into a large bowl, adding any bran remaining in the sifter back into the bowl. Stir flour mixture and yogurt alternately into egg mixture. Stir in the sesame seeds, grated lemon peel and juice. Spoon into prepared pan and smooth the surface.

Bake about 1 hour or until golden and a skewer inserted in the center comes out clean. Cool on a wire rack. Cut into 14 slices.

Makes 1 loaf.

Store in an airtight container. Suitable for freezing.

These days, everyone should try to eat a lowfat, high-fiber diet, so don't keep these recipes to yourself!

Each slice contains:

				Exchanges:	
Calories	152	Total Fat	8g	Bread	0.7
Protein	4g	Saturated Fat	1g	Fruit	0.2
Carbohydrates	16g	Cholesterol	31mg	Milk	0.1
Fiber	1g	Sodium	195mg	Meat	0.1
				Fat	1.5

Farmhouse Fruit Scones

You may need to use all of the egg and milk if the mixture seems dry because this will vary with the flour used. Use a little extra milk for brushing the tops of the scones before baking.

They are best eaten the same day or may be frozen.

1-1/4	cups all-purpose flour
1/2	cup whole-wheat flour
2-1/2	teaspoons baking powder
1/2	teaspoon salt
3	tablespoons soft margarine
1/4	cup sugar
1/2	cup raisins or currants
1	egg, beaten with enough nonfat milk to make 1/2 cup
	Milk for brushing

Preheat oven to 425F (220C). Sift the flours, baking powder and salt into a large bowl, adding any bran remaining in the sifter back into the bowl. Cut in the margarine until the mixture resembles bread crumbs. Stir in the sugar and raisins. Gradually add enough of the egg and milk mixture to form a soft dough.

Knead the mixture on a lightly floured surface and roll out to about 1/2-inch thickness. Cut into 2-inch rounds, rerolling the trimmings. Place on a floured baking sheet and brush the tops with a little milk. Bake 10 to 12 minutes or until puffed and golden. Serve warm, or cool on a wire rack.

Makes about 14 scones.

Each scone contains:

				Exchanges:	
Calories	116	Total Fat	3g	Bread	0.7
Protein	3g	Saturated Fat	1g	Fruit	0.5
Carbohydrates	20g	Cholesterol	15mg	Meat	0.1
Fiber	1g	Sodium	171mg	Fat	0.5

Apricot-and-Raisin Bread

A moist fruit loaf that is high in fiber and low in fat.

Wrap well and store in an airtight container. It will keep 3 or 4 days—or it can be frozen.

1	cup all-bran cereal
4	oz. dried apricots, chopped
3/4	cup raisins
1	cup strong hot tea
3/4	cup all-purpose flour
2	teaspoons baking powder
2	eggs, beaten

Preheat oven to 350F (175C). Grease a 9 x 5-inch loaf pan and line with waxed paper. Place the cereal, apricots, raisins and tea in a bowl and mix well. Let stand 15 to 20 minutes. Stir in the flour, baking powder and eggs and mix well. Spoon into prepared pan and smooth the surface.

Bake 45 to 50 minutes or until a skewer inserted in the center comes out clean. Cool on a wire rack. Cut into 14 slices.

Makes 1 loaf.

Each slice contains:

				Exchanges:	
Calories	96	Total Fat	1g	Bread	0.5
Protein	3g	Saturated Fat	0g	Fruit	0.8
Carbohydrates	22g	Cholesterol	30mg	Meat	0.1
Fiber	3g	Sodium	132mg	Fat	0.1

Cherry-and-Walnut Bread

This makes delicious toast. Top with fat-free cream cheese.

When making quick breads in which the fat and sugar are creamed together, you can usually reduce the amount of sugar by half, as I have in this recipe.

1/2	cup soft margarine
1/4	cup sugar
1	egg, lightly beaten
2	cups all-purpose flour
1	tablespoon baking powder
1	teaspoon pumpkin- or apple-pie spice
	Pinch of salt
1/2	cup chopped walnuts
4	oz. glacé cherries, rinsed, dried and chopped
3/4	cup nonfat milk

Preheat oven to 350F (175C). Grease a 9 x 5-inch loaf pan and line with waxed paper. Beat the margarine and sugar together until pale and creamy. Gradually beat in the egg. Sift the flour, baking powder, spice and salt together into a large bowl. Stir in the walnuts and cherries. Stir the flour mixture and milk alternately into the creamed mixture to make a smooth batter. Pour the mixture into prepared pan.

Bake 1-1/4 hours or until a skewer inserted in the center comes out clean. Cool in the pan 10 minutes before turning out on to a wire rack to cool completely. Cut into 12 to 14 slices.

Makes 1 loaf.

For 12 slices, each slice contains:

				Exchanges:	
Calories	234	Total Fat	11g	Bread	1.0
Protein	4g	Saturated Fat	2g	Fruit	0.3
Carbohydrates	30g	Cholesterol	18mg	Milk	0.1
Fiber	1g	Sodium	197mg	Meat	0.1
				Fat	1.6

Buttermilk Cornbread

Southerners use buttermilk. As a rule, you can use nonfat milk as well. For a complete meal, place a piece of cornbread on a plate, and top with your favorite bean or chili dish.

1	cup cornmeal
1/2	cup all-purpose flour
1/2	teaspoon baking soda
1	teaspoon baking powder
1	teaspoon sugar
2	tablespoons canola oil
1	egg, lightly beaten
1	cup buttermilk

Preheat oven to 450F (230C). Grease an 8-inch-square baking pan. Combine cornmeal, flour, soda, baking powder and sugar in a medium bowl. Combine oil, egg and buttermilk in another bowl. Add to cornmeal mixture and stir just until moistened. Pour into prepared pan. Bake 20 to 25 minutes or until golden brown. Cut into 8 rectangles.

Makes 8 pieces.

Each piece contains:

				Exchanges:	
Calories	146	Total Fat	5g	Bread	1.1
Protein	4g	Saturated Fat	1g	Milk	0.2
Carbohydrates	22g	Cholesterol	28mg	Meat	0.1
Fiber	2g	Sodium	165mg	Fat	0.7

Whole-wheat Bread

Easy-blend dried yeast should be stirred into the dry ingredients before adding the water, unlike fresh or traditional dried yeast, which needs to be added to liquid first.

Best eaten the same day. Suitable for freezing.

2	cups bread flour
1-1/2	cups whole-wheat flour
1	tablespoon sugar
2	teaspoons salt
1	pkg. (1/4-oz.) active dried yeast
1/4	cup soft margarine
1-1/4	cups nonfat milk, heated to 125F (55C)

Place the flours, sugar, salt and yeast in a large bowl. Cut in the margarine and add enough milk to make a soft dough. Turn out on a lightly floured board and knead 10 to 15 minutes until smooth and elastic.

Place in an oiled bowl, cover and let rise in a warm place until doubled in size, about 1 hour. Punch down dough. Let rest 10 minutes. Grease a 9 x 5-inch loaf pan. Shape dough into a loaf and place in prepared pan. Let rise in a warm place until the dough is almost to the top of the pan, about 45 minutes. Preheat oven to 350F (175C).

Bake 50 minutes or until browned. Cool on a wire rack. Cut into about 16 slices.

Makes 1 loaf.

Each slice contains:

				Exchanges:	
Calories	125	Total Fat	4g	Bread	1.1
Protein	4g	Saturated Fat	1g	Fruit	0.1
Carbohydrates	20g	Cholesterol	0mg	Milk	0.1
Fiber	2g	Sodium	304mg	Fat	0.6

Hot Cross Buns

*You needn't wait for Easter
to fix these buns. Enjoy
them year-round.*

To make the buns in advance, allow to cool unglazed before freezing. Heat thawed buns in a hot oven 2 to 3 minutes to warm, then glaze as in the recipe before serving.

2-3/4	cups bread flour
1	cup whole-wheat flour
1	teaspoon salt
1	teaspoon apple-pie spice
1/2	teaspoon ground cinnamon
1/2	cup soft margarine
1	(1/4-oz.) pkg. active dried yeast
1/4	cup sugar
1	cup dried currants
1/2	cup nonfat milk, heated to 125F (55C)
1	egg, beaten
1/4	cup warm water

Glaze

1	tablespoon reduced-sugar apricot jam
3	tablespoons water

Sift the flours, salt and spices into a large bowl, adding any bran remaining in the sifter back to the bowl. Cut in the margarine. Stir in the yeast, sugar and currants. Make a well in the center and add the milk, egg and enough water to form a soft dough. Turn out dough on a lightly floured surface and knead until smooth and elastic. Place in an oiled bowl, cover with plastic wrap and let rise in a warm place until doubled in size, 1 to 1-1/2 hours.

Punch down the dough and shape into 14 balls. Let rest 10 minutes. Grease 2 baking sheets. Place well apart on prepared baking sheets and flatten slightly. Cover with plastic wrap and let rise 30 minutes.

Preheat oven to 400F (205C). Remove the plastic wrap and slash a cross in each bun. Bake 15 to 20 minutes. Heat the jam and water together over low heat and use to brush over the buns while still hot. Cool on a wire rack.

Makes 14 buns.

Each bun contains:

Calories	222	Total Fat	8g	
Protein	5g	Saturated Fat	1g	
Carbohydrates	35g	Cholesterol	15mg	
Fiber	2g	Sodium	225mg	

Exchanges:

Bread	1.4
Vegetable	0.1
Fruit	0.7
Meat	0.1
Fat	1.3

Bread Porcupines

It doesn't take very long to make the porcupine shapes and you will find it was worth the effort when you present these to your children! They might help you shape the dough.

1-1/2	cups whole-wheat flour
2	cups bread flour
1	tablespoon sugar
1-1/2	teaspoons salt
1	pkg. (1/4-oz.) active dried yeast
1	cup 2% lowfat milk, warmed to 125F (55C)
28	currants or raisins
	Milk for glazing

In a large bowl, mix together the whole-wheat flour, 1-1/2 cups of the bread flour, sugar, salt and yeast. Pour in the milk and mix to make a firm dough, adding additional flour as needed. Knead until smooth and springy. Place the dough in a bowl, cover with a clean towel, and let rise in a warm place 1-1/2 hours or until doubled in size.

Remove the dough from the bowl and knead again 2 minutes. Cut into 14 pieces and form into oval shapes with a pointed nose. Snip the top of the dough with scissors to make quills. Press 2 currants into the dough to make eyes. Cover again and let rise 20 to 30 minutes or until doubled in size. Preheat oven to 425F (220C). Brush porcupines with a little milk. Bake 10 to 15 minutes or until golden brown. Serve warm.

Makes 14 porcupines.

Each porcupine contains:

				Exchanges:	
Calories	126	Total Fat	1g	Bread	1.3
Protein	5g	Saturated Fat	0g	Vegetable	0.1
Carbohydrates	25g	Cholesterol	1mg	Fruit	0.2
Fiber	2g	Sodium	241mg	Milk	0.1
				Fat	0.1

Cakes and Cookies

Many people are concerned that they will be unable to eat cakes and cookies once they have been diagnosed with diabetes. It is still possible to eat them occasionally as part of an overall healthful diet. The recipes in this section have been developed using as little sugar as possible, together with high-fiber ingredients such as whole-wheat flour or oats as the main ingredients. Some recipes have no added sugar but rely upon the natural sweetness of dried fruit. Because of the reduced sugar and fat content, the cakes and cookies are best eaten within a few days or they may be frozen in convenient portions and used as required. This ensures that they are eaten at their best.

Carrot Cake

A pretty two-layer cake that can also be made in a 13 x 9-inch pan and cut into 24 squares—ideal for a picnic.

Best eaten within 2 days. Suitable for freezing.

2	cups all-purpose flour
1	tablespoon baking powder
1-1/2	teaspoons baking soda
1-1/2	teaspoons pumpkin-pie spice mix
1/4	cup packed light brown sugar
3	eggs, separated
1	small ripe banana, mashed
1	large carrot, peeled and grated (1/2 cup)
1/3	cup vegetable oil
1/2	cup buttermilk
1	teaspoon vanilla extract
1	teaspoon banana extract
2	small bananas, sliced
1	cup frozen whipped nondairy dessert topping
	Dash nutmeg

Preheat oven to 350F (175C). Lightly grease two 8-inch baking pans. Stir together flour, baking powder, baking soda, spice mix and sugar in a bowl. Combine egg yolks, banana, carrot, oil and buttermilk. Stir into dry ingredients and beat well.

Whip eggs whites and fold into mixture. Pour into prepared pans. Bake 30 to 35 minutes or until a skewer inserted into the center comes out clean. Allow to cool in the pan a few minutes, then turn out onto a wire rack to cool completely. Place half the sliced bananas on one layer, top with half of the

Each serving (two slices) contains:

				Exchanges:	
Calories	212	Total Fat	9g	Bread	0.9
Protein	4g	Saturated Fat	1g	Vegetable	0.1
Carbohydrates	28g	Cholesterol	53mg	Fruit	0.6
Fiber	1g	Sodium	279mg	Milk	0.1
				Meat	0.2
				Fat	1.3

frozen whipped topping. Place second layer on top, use remaining banana slices and topping as before. Sprinkle with a dash of nutmeg, if desired.

Makes 12 servings. If using a 13 x 9-inch pan, cut into 24 squares.

Pinolata

This Italian dessert cake is particularly nice served with a fresh fruit salad.

2	eggs
1/4	cup sugar
	Grated peel of 1 lemon
3/4	cup soft margarine
2-1/4	cups all-purpose flour
1/2	cup dry sherry
1	teaspoon vanilla extract
2	oz. pine nuts

Preheat oven to 350F (175C). Grease a deep 9-inch cake pan and line bottom with waxed paper. Whisk the eggs and sugar together until pale and creamy. Beat in the lemon peel, margarine, flour, sherry and vanilla. Mix until well blended and smooth. Pour into prepared pan. Sprinkle the pine nuts over the top. Bake 30 minutes or until a skewer inserted into the center comes out clean. Serve warm.

Makes 12 servings.

Pine Nuts

Buy pine nuts in small quantities and use them up quickly. They go rancid rapidly because of their high fat content. Store unused portion in the freezer.

Each serving contains:

				Exchanges:	
Calories	247	Total Fat	15g	Bread	1.1
Protein	5g	Saturated Fat	3g	Fruit	0.3
Carbohydrates	23g	Cholesterol	35mg	Meat	0.2
Fiber	1g	Sodium	117mg	Fat	2.8

Spiced Mandarin Gâteau

This elegant dessert is perfect for entertaining. I use all-purpose flour for the cake because I find it gives a better result than whole-wheat flour. However, if you prefer, you could use half whole-wheat and half all-purpose flour.

4	eggs
1/2	cup plus 2 teaspoons sugar
1	cup all-purpose flour
1/4	teaspoon ground ginger
1/4	teaspoon ground cinnamon
1/4	cup margarine, melted and cooled

Filling

1	cup whipping cream
2	tablespoons granulated artificial sweetener
1	(11-oz.) can mandarin segments in natural juice, drained

Preheat oven to 375F (190C). Grease a 13 x 9-inch baking pan. Using an electric mixer, beat the eggs and the 1/2 cup sugar together 5 minutes or until pale and thick and the beaters leave a trail in the mixture for a few seconds when lifted.

Sift the flour and spices together. Fold carefully into the egg mixture. Finally, fold in the margarine. Pour the mixture into prepared pan. Bake 15 to 20 minutes or until cake springs back when lightly touched with a fingertip.

Sprinkle a sheet of waxed paper with the 2 teaspoons sugar. Turn out cake on the waxed paper and remove the lining paper. Trim cake edges very thinly and roll up with the clean paper inside. Cool completely on a wire rack.

Beat whipping cream and sweetener until stiff. Unroll the cake carefully and spread with 3/4 of the cream. Reserve 8 mandarin segments for decoration, arrange remaining segments over the cream, reroll the sponge carefully, sprinkle with a little sweetener (optional), and place on a serving dish.

Pipe the reserved cream down the center of the roll and decorate with the remaining mandarin segments. Refrigerate until ready to serve.

Makes 10 to 12 servings.

For 10 servings, each serving contains:				Exchanges:	
				Bread	0.6
Calories	252	Total Fat	16g	Fruit	1.0
Protein	5g	Saturated Fat	7g	Milk	0.1
Carbohydrates	24g	Cholesterol	118mg	Meat	0.4
Fiber	1g	Sodium	78mg	Fat	2.8

Apricot Upside-down Cake

A variation on the traditional pineapple upside-down cake. The sugar content has been reduced by using fruit canned in juice rather than syrup.

1	(14-oz.) can apricot halves in natural juice
2	tablespoons granulated artificial sweetener
1/4	cup soft margarine
1/3	cup sugar
1	egg
1-3/4	cups cake flour, sifted
1	teaspoon baking powder
1/2	teaspoon vanilla extract
1/4	cup nonfat milk

You can vary the fruit in an upside-down cake to suit whatever is at hand. Peach slices or halves are a good choice. Try pear halves or pitted cherries; they are especially delicious when a little cocoa powder is added to the cake batter.

Preheat oven to 350F (175C). Grease a 9-inch cake pan and line with waxed paper. Drain the apricot halves, reserving the juice. Arrange the apricots flat side down in the bottom of prepared pan. Mix 1/4 of the apricot juice with the sweetener and spoon over the apricots.

Beat margarine and sugar together until creamy. Beat in eggs, one at a time. Sift together flour and baking powder. Beat into creamed mixture alternately with milk.

Spoon the batter over the apricots. Bake in the center of the oven about 35 minutes or until golden and firm to the touch. Turn out on a serving plate and remove the lining paper. Serve warm.

Makes 10 servings.

Each serving contains:

				Exchanges:	
Calories	157	Total Fat	5g	Bread	0.8
Protein	3g	Saturated Fat	1g	Fruit	0.8
Carbohydrates	25g	Cholesterol	21mg	Meat	0.1
Fiber	1g	Sodium	90mg	Fat	1.0

Yellow Cake

This versatile cake can be used as the basis for many recipes, from elaborate birthday cakes to simple cupcakes. You can add many different flavors, such as cocoa powder, lemon or orange peel or coffee.

Store in an airtight container. Best eaten within 2 to 3 days. Suitable for freezing.

Tip

If using pure-fruit spread or reduced-sugar jam to fill the cake, remember to count the extra carbohydrate and calories.

A pretty finishing touch is to sift a little granulated sweetener over a paper doily on top of the cake. When the doily is lifted, it leaves a lacy pattern.

1/2	cup soft margarine
2/3	cup sugar
2	eggs, separated
1-3/4	cups cake flour, sifted
2	teaspoons baking powder
1/4	teaspoon salt
1/2	teaspoon vanilla extract
1/2	cup nonfat milk

Preheat oven to 375F (190C). Grease two (9-inch) cake pans and line bottoms with waxed paper. Beat margarine and sugar together until creamy. Beat in egg yolks, one at a time. Sift together flour, baking powder and salt. Beat into creamed mixture alternately with milk. Beat egg whites until stiff but not dry. Fold into cake batter. Divide batter between prepared pans.

Bake in the center of the oven about 25 minutes or until golden and firm to the touch. Turn out and cool on a wire rack.

Makes 2 layers, 8 to 10 servings.

Exchanges:

For 8 servings, each serving contains:

Calories	267	Total Fat	13g	Bread	0.9
Protein	4g	Saturated Fat	2g	Fruit	1.1
Carbohydrates	34g	Cholesterol	53mg	Milk	0.1
Fiber	0g	Sodium	286mg	Meat	0.2
				Fat	2.4

Coconut-and-Cherry Fingers

Whether you call these a cookie or cake, the result is delicious. Coconut adds a crunchiness and the cherries give both color and flavor.

These will keep up to two days in an airtight tin or may be frozen for longer storage.

1-3/4	cups all-purpose flour
2	teaspoons baking powder
1/2	cup soft margarine
1/3	cup sugar
2/3	cup shredded coconut
4	oz. glacé cherries, washed, dried and chopped
1	egg, lightly beaten
2	tablespoons lemon juice
3/4	cup nonfat milk

Preheat oven to 325F. Grease an 11 x 7-inch baking pan and line bottom with waxed paper. Mix the flour and baking powder together in a large bowl. Cut in the margarine until the mixture resembles bread crumbs. Stir in the sugar, coconut and cherries. Stir in the egg and lemon juice and enough milk to make a soft batter. Spoon into prepared pan. Bake 40 to 45 minutes or until golden brown and firm. Turn out onto a wire rack. When cooled, cut into fingers.

Makes 16.

Each serving contains:

				Exchanges:	
Calories	167	Total Fat	8g	Bread	0.6
Protein	2g	Saturated Fat	2g	Fruit	0.4
Carbohydrates	23g	Cholesterol	13mg	Meat	0.1
Fiber	1g	Sodium	118mg	Fat	1.4

Chocolate Squares

Decorate these squares with a little icing for a children's party.

3	tablespoons cocoa powder, sifted
2	tablespoons boiling water
1-3/4	cups all-purpose flour
2	teaspoons baking powder
1	cup soft margarine
1/2	cup sugar
3	eggs, beaten
3	tablespoons nonfat milk
1	teaspoon vanilla extract

Preheat oven to 350F (175C). Grease a 9 x 9-inch baking pan and line the bottom with waxed paper. Stir the cocoa powder and the boiling water together until smooth.

Sift the flour and baking powder together and beat in the cocoa mixture with the margarine, sugar, eggs, milk and vanilla. Beat until smooth. Spoon into prepared pan. Bake 25 to 30 minutes or until top springs back when pressed. Cool in the pan before turning out onto a wire rack to cool completely.

Makes 16 squares.

Each square contains:

Calories	194	Total Fat	13g	Bread	0.6
Protein	3g	Saturated Fat	2g	Fruit	0.4
Carbohydrates	18g	Cholesterol	40mg	Meat	0.2
Fiber	1g	Sodium	164mg	Fat	2.4

Exchanges:

Shortbread

Shortbread is a traditional family favorite. However, because it is high in fat and calories, I suggest including it in your diet as an occasional treat, rather than an everyday snack.

1	cup soft margarine
2	cups all-purpose flour
1/4	cup sugar

Best eaten within 2 to 3 days.

I like to pack these in a small tin and give as a hostess gift. They're always well received.

Cut the margarine into the flour until the mixture resembles fine bread crumbs. Stir in the sugar and knead together until a soft dough is formed, leaving the bowl clean. Press into an 8-inch round pan and smooth the top. Flute the edges and prick all over with a fork. Mark into 8 portions. Chill 30 minutes.

Preheat oven to 300F (150C). Bake 50 to 60 minutes. Leave in the pan for 10 minutes before cooling completely on a wire rack. Sprinkle with a little granulated artificial sweetener if desired. Wrap in foil and store in an airtight container.

Makes 8 servings.

Each serving contains:

Calories	341	Total Fat	23g	Bread	1.4
Protein	3g	Saturated Fat	4g	Fruit	0.4
Carbohydrates	30g	Cholesterol	0mg	Fat	4.5
Fiber	1g	Sodium	210mg		

Exchanges:

Cherry-and-Raisin Cake

A light fruitcake that is delicious as an afternoon snack—or served with a cup of tea.

1-1/4	cups all-purpose flour
3/4	cup whole-wheat flour
4	oz. glacé cherries, rinsed and dried
3/4	cup raisins
3/4	cup soft margarine
1/4	cup sugar
1	teaspoon baking powder
3	eggs, beaten
	Grated peel and juice of 1 lemon
3	tablespoons nonfat milk

Preheat oven to 350F (175C). Grease an 8-inch cake pan and line bottom with waxed paper. Stir flours together. Coarsely chop the cherries and mix together with the raisins and 1/3 of the flour mixture.

Beat the margarine and sugar together until pale and creamy. Add the eggs and beat well. Beat in remaining flour and baking powder. Stir in the cherry mixture, lemon peel and juice, and milk. Spoon into prepared pan and level the top. Bake 50 to 60 minutes or until a skewer inserted into the center of the cake comes out clean. Allow to cool in the pan 10 minutes before turning out on to a wire rack to cool completely.

Makes 12 to 16 servings.

For 12 servings, each serving contains: **Exchanges:**

Calories	271	Total Fat	13g	Bread	0.9
Protein	5g	Saturated Fat	2g	Fruit	0.8
Carbohydrates	36g	Cholesterol	53mg	Meat	0.2
Fiber	2g	Sodium	155mg	Fat	2.4

Spiced Apple-and-Almond Cake

For a more festive look, serve with a dollop of whipped cream or topping.

3	Granny Smith apples (1 lb.), peeled, cored and coarsely chopped
1	tablespoon lemon juice
3	tablespoons water
1-1/2	cups all-purpose flour
1/2	cup whole-wheat flour
2	teaspoons baking powder
1	teaspoon baking soda
1/2	cup soft margarine
1/2	cup packed light-brown sugar
2	eggs, beaten
1/2	teaspoon almond extract
1/4	cup chopped almonds
1/4	teaspoon ground cloves
1	teaspoons ground cinnamon
1/2	teaspoon ground nutmeg
1/4	cup milk

Preheat oven to 350F (175C). Grease an 8-inch-round cake pan and line the bottom. Place all ingredients in a food processor or mixer bowl. Blend for a few seconds until thoroughly combined. Spoon the batter into prepared pan.

Each slice contains:

Calories	163	Total Fat	8g	Bread	0.7
Protein	3g	Saturated Fat	1g	Fruit	0.6
Carbohydrates	21g	Cholesterol	27mg	Meat	0.2
Fiber	2g	Sodium	189mg	Fat	1.4

Exchanges:

Bake 50 to 60 minutes or until a skewer inserted in the center comes out clean. Cool in the pan 10 minutes before turning out onto a wire rack to cool completely. Cut into slices.

Makes 16 slices.

Old-fashioned Gingerbread

For added color and flavor, spoon fresh berries or peaches over each serving.

2	cups all-purpose flour
2	teaspoons ground ginger
1	teaspoon baking soda
1/2	cup soft margarine
1/3	cup packed brown sugar
1/4	cup molasses
1-1/4	cups nonfat milk
1	egg, lightly beaten
1	teaspoon vanilla extract

Preheat oven to 325F (165C). Grease a 9-inch-square baking pan and line the bottom with waxed paper. Mix together the flour, ginger and soda into a bowl. Add the remaining ingredients to the bowl and beat until thoroughly mixed.

Pour into prepared pan. Bake 50 to 55 minutes or until a skewer inserted into the center comes out clean. Allow to cool in the pan for a few minutes before turning out to cool completely on a wire rack. Cut into 16 squares.

Makes 16 servings.

Each square contains:

				Exchanges:	
Calories	145	Total Fat	6g	Bread	0.7
Protein	3g	Saturated Fat	1g	Fruit	0.4
Carbohydrates	19g	Cholesterol	14mg	Milk	0.1
Fiber	1g	Sodium	148mg	Meat	0.1
				Fat	1.2

German Plum Coffeecake

Because it's not overly sweet, the plum flavor is more pronounced.

The deep-red color of plums is very attractive. You can easily substitute apples, peaches or apricots. Delicious served warm or cold.

1/3	cup soft margarine
1	egg
1/2	cup milk
1	tablespoon baking powder
2	tablespoons sugar
2	cups all-purpose flour
1	teaspoon vanilla extract
1	lb. fresh plums, cut in eighths
1	tablespoon sugar
1	teaspoon ground cinnamon
1/4	teaspoon ground nutmeg

Preheat oven to 400F (205C). Grease a 9-inch-square baking pan.

Beat together margarine, egg and milk. Stir in baking powder, 2 tablespoons sugar, flour and vanilla.

Spoon mixture into prepared pan. Press plum pieces into dough making a pretty pattern. Combine 1 tablespoon sugar, cinnamon and nutmeg. Sprinkle over plums. Bake 30 to 35 minutes. Cool at least 10 minutes before serving.

Makes 16 servings.

Each serving contains:

				Exchanges:	
Calories	125	Total Fat	5g	Bread	0.7
Protein	3g	Saturated Fat	1g	Fruit	0.4
Carbohydrates	19g	Cholesterol	14mg	Meat	0.1
Fiber	1g	Sodium	111mg	Fat	0.8

Tropical Island Cookies

If you prefer, substitute 4 teaspoons of orange or lemon peel for the extract.

2	cups all-purpose flour
2	teaspoons baking powder
1/2	cup sugar
1-1/2	cups shredded coconut
1	whole egg, lightly beaten
1	egg white, lightly beaten
4	teaspoons rum extract
1/3	cup soft margarine

Preheat oven to 400F (205C). Grease a baking sheet. Combine the flour, baking powder, sugar and coconut in a bowl. Gradually add the egg, extract and margarine to the flour mixture and mix to a firm dough. (You may not need to add all of the margarine.)

Shape the cookie dough into 24 round balls and place 2 inches apart on the baking sheet. Bake 10 to 15 minutes or until golden brown. Cool on a wire rack.

Makes 24 cookies.

Each cookie contains:

					Exchanges:	
Calories	110	Total Fat	5g	Bread	0.5
Protein	2g	Saturated Fat	2g	Fruit	0.5
Carbohydrates	15g	Cholesterol	9mg	Meat	0.1
Fiber	1g	Sodium	74mg	Fat	0.8

Lemon-and-Almond Cake

Sliced lemons on top give an attractive finish.

1	cup soft margarine
1/2	cup sugar
3	eggs, beaten
1-1/2	cups all-purpose flour
2	teaspoons baking powder
1/3	cup (about 2 oz.) ground almonds
	Grated peel and juice of 1 large lemon
1/2	teaspoon almond extract

To finish

2	lemons
1	tablespoon reduced-sugar marmalade
1	tablespoon water

I found the combination of lemons and almonds very refreshing compared to traditional recipes of this type, which tend to be very sweet.

Preheat oven to 325F (165C). Grease an 8-inch springform pan and line the bottom with waxed paper. Place all the cake ingredients in a large bowl. Beat with an electric mixer 2 to 3 minutes or until light and fluffy. Turn the mixture into prepared pan and smooth the top.

Pare entire peel and pith from lemons, then slice into thin rounds. Arrange on top of the cake.

Bake 50 to 60 minutes until golden and firm. Cool in the pan 5 minutes, then release the sides and cool on a wire rack. Warm marmalade and water together. Sieve and brush over the top of warm cake.

Makes 14 to 16 slices.

Each slice contains:

				Exchanges:	
Calories	233	Total Fat	16g	Bread	0.6
Protein	4g	Saturated Fat	3g	Fruit	0.5
Carbohydrates	19g	Cholesterol	46mg	Meat	0.3
Fiber	1g	Sodium	186mg	Fat	3.0

Pound Cake

A traditional cake enlivened with fresh lemon. For a change, substitute orange or grapefruit peel for the lemon peel.

1/2	cup soft margarine
1/2	cup sugar
3	eggs
1-1/2	cups all-purpose flour
1-1/2	teaspoons baking powder
1	tablespoon finely grated lemon peel
1	teaspoon vanilla extract

Best eaten within 1 to 2 days. Suitable for freezing. Store in an airtight container.

Preheat oven to 325F (165C). Grease a 9 x 5-inch loaf pan and line with waxed paper. Beat margarine and sugar until light and creamy. Beat in eggs, one at a time, beating well after each addition. Beat in flour, baking powder, lemon peel and vanilla. Spoon batter into prepared pan and level the top.

Bake about 1 hour or until a skewer inserted in center of cake comes out clean. Cool in the pan for a few minutes before turning out to complete cooling on a wire rack.

Makes 16 slices.

Each serving contains:				*Exchanges:*	
Calories	132	Total Fat	7g	Bread	0.5
Protein	2g	Saturated Fat	1g	Fruit	0.4
Carbohydrates	15g	Cholesterol	40mg	Meat	0.2
Fiber	0g	Sodium	99mg	Fat	1.2

Orange-and-Ginger Cookies

Sprinkle the cookies with a little granulated artificial sweetener when baked for a sweeter taste.

1/2	cup soft margarine
1/4	cup sugar
1	egg, beaten
1-1/4	cups quick-cooking oats
1	cup all-purpose flour
1/2	teaspoon baking powder
1/2	teaspoon salt
1	tablespoon ground ginger
2	teaspoons vanilla extract
1	tablespoon orange extract
2	tablespoons orange zest
1	to 2 tablespoons milk (optional)

Preheat oven to 375F (190C). Grease 2 baking sheets. Beat together margarine, sugar and egg. Add remaining ingredients and stir until combined. Add milk if batter is too stiff. Drop mixture by heaping tablespoonfuls about 2 inches apart on prepared baking sheets. Flatten slightly with a fork. Bake 12 to 15 minutes or until golden and just firm to the touch. Cool on a wire rack.

Makes 24 cookies.

Each serving contains:

Calories	67	Total Fat	4g	*Exchanges:*	
Protein	1g	Saturated Fat	1g	Bread	0.5
Carbohydrates	7g	Cholesterol	9mg		
Fiber	0g	Sodium	90mg		

Date-and-Apricot Bars

These old-fashioned treats are a bit crumbly and a hit with everyone in the family.

Enjoy the natural sweetness of these dried fruits. If you wish, substitute dried apples for the apricot. Best eaten within 1 to 2 days. Suitable for freezing.

3/4	cup (6 oz.) pitted dates, chopped
2/3	cup (4 oz.) dried apricots, chopped
1/2	cup water
1-1/2	cups all-purpose flour
1-1/3	cups quick-cooking oats
1	teaspoon baking powder
1/4	cup packed light-brown sugar
3/4	cup soft margarine
1-1/2	teaspoons vanilla extract

Place the dates and apricots in a saucepan with the water and simmer 10 minutes or until soft and the mixture forms a paste. Let cool.

Preheat oven to 375F (190C). Grease a 13 x 9-inch baking pan and line the bottom with waxed paper. Combine flour, oats, baking powder and sugar in a bowl. Cut in margarine and vanilla until mixture resembles coarse crumbs. Press half the mixture into the bottom of prepared pan. Spoon the date and apricot mixture over the top. Spoon the remaining oat mixture over to cover evenly and press down with your fingers. Bake 30 minutes or until lightly browned. Cool in the pan 10 minutes. Mark into 18 bars and cool completely on a wire rack.

Makes 18 bars.

Each bar contains:

				Exchanges:	
Calories	150	Total Fat	8g	Bread	0.5
Protein	2g	Saturated Fat	1g	Fruit	0.7
Carbohydrates	19g	Cholesterol	0mg	Fat	1.5
Fiber	1g	Sodium	92mg		

Raisin Cookies

Younger children will enjoy making these cookies. They may need some help from an adult to bake them, especially when they are handling hot equipment.

2	cups all-purpose flour
1	teaspoon baking powder
1	teaspoon ground cinnamon
1	teaspoon allspice
1/2	cup soft margarine
1/3	cup sugar
3/4	cup dried currants or raisins
1	egg, beaten
1	teaspoon vanilla extract
5	tablespoons nonfat milk

Preheat oven to 400F (205C). Grease a baking sheet. Place the flour, baking powder and cinnamon in a bowl. Cut in the margarine until the mixture looks like bread crumbs. Stir in the sugar and the currants or raisins. Combine the egg, vanilla and milk in a small bowl and beat together with a fork. Pour into the currant mixture in the bowl. Mix well. The mixture will be sticky.

Drop cookie dough in 14 spoonfuls 2 inches apart on the baking sheet. Bake 10 to 15 minutes or until golden brown. Cool on a wire rack.

Makes 14 cookies.

Each cookie contains:

				Exchanges:	
Calories	171	Total Fat	7g	Bread	0.8
Protein	3g	Saturated Fat	1g	Fruit	0.6
Carbohydrates	25g	Cholesterol	15mg	Meat	0.1
Fiber	1g	Sodium	94mg	Fat	1.3

Desserts

I've used artificial sweeteners wherever possible for these recipes to cut down on the sugar or simple carbohydrate content. Sweeteners are also useful to sweeten drinks and sweet sauces.

Once you are accustomed to less sugar, the true fruit flavor becomes the focus of dessert.

Lemon-and-Raisin Cheesecake

This baked cheesecake has a lovely lemon flavor that complements the raisins. When I served this to guests, they didn't realize it was not sweetened with sugar!

5	oz. golden raisins
	Finely grated peel and juice of 3 lemons
3/4	cup all-purpose flour
3/4	cup whole-wheat flour
1/4	cup soft margarine
2 to 3	tablespoons water
1	tablespoon cornstarch
2	(8-oz.) pkgs. fat-free cream cheese, softened
2 to 3	tablespoons granulated artificial sweetener
3	eggs, beaten
1	teaspoon vanilla extract

Place the raisins, lemon peel and juice in a bowl and let stand 30 minutes.

Sift the flours into a bowl. Add any bran remaining in the sifter back into the bowl. Cut in the margarine until the mixture resembles fine bread crumbs. Add enough cold water to mix to a soft dough. Shape into a ball, cover and refrigerate 30 minutes.

Roll out pastry on a lightly floured surface to line the bottom and sides of a 9-inch-round tart pan with a removable bottom. Chill 15 minutes. Preheat oven to 400F (205C). Line pastry with foil, fill with dried beans and bake 5 minutes. Remove the foil and beans and bake another 5 minutes. Reduce the oven temperature to 325F (165C).

Beat the cornstarch, cream cheese, sweetener, eggs, vanilla, raisins and lemon juice together in a large bowl. Beat well to mix thoroughly. Pour the mixture into pastry shell and bake 45 minutes or until firm and golden. Allow to cool. Run a knife around the edge and remove from the pan. Chill before serving. Sprinkle with a little sweetener to serve, if desired.

Makes 10 servings.

Each serving contains:				*Exchanges*:	
Calories	216	Total Fat	6g	Bread	0.9
Protein	11g	Saturated Fat	1g	Fruit	0.7
Carbohydrates	29g	Cholesterol	67mg	Meat	0.3
Fiber	2g	Sodium	283mg	Fat	1.1

Strawberry Creams

I have made this recipe using a lowfat evaporated milk that I chilled overnight, and it gave a similar result with no difference in taste. If you can buy the low-fat evaporated milk, it will yield about half the amount of fat per serving.

1   (0.3-oz.) pkg. sugar-free strawberry gelatin dessert
1   cup boiling water
1   (12-oz.) can evaporated lowfat or whole milk,
    chilled overnight
    Sliced fresh strawberries and mint sprigs to decorate

Dissolve the gelatin dessert in the boiling water in a medium bowl. Set aside until cooled. Meanwhile, using an electric mixer, beat the evaporated milk in a chilled bowl until thickened and doubled in volume. Fold the cooled gelatin mixture into the milk until thoroughly blended. Pour into 4 (1-cup) dessert molds or individual dishes. It won't all fit at first, but as the mixture settles, you will be able to fill up the molds with the remaining mixture. Chill about 3 hours or until set. Dip the molds in hot water 10 seconds and gently turn out on serving plates. Decorate with sliced fresh strawberries and mint sprigs.

Makes 4 servings.

Mandarin Creams

When strawberries are not in season, substitute an orange gelatin dessert mix and decorate with a well-drained can of mandarin orange segments in natural juice.

Each serving contains:

Calories	93	Total Fat	2g	Fruit	0.2
Protein	8g	Saturated Fat	1g	Milk	0.9
Carbohydrates	12g	Cholesterol	7mg		
Fiber	0g	Sodium	150mg		

Exchanges:

Rhubarb-and-Ginger Fool

Ginger adds spicy flavor to this easy dessert. It is low in calories and fat.

1	lb. rhubarb, trimmed and cut into chunks
1	tablespoon finely grated fresh ginger
3	tablespoons water
3 to 4	tablespoons granulated artificial sweetener
1	cup nonfat milk
2	tablespoons cornstarch
1	teaspoon vanilla extract

Place the rhubarb, ginger and water into a saucepan over low heat. Cover and simmer 5 to 10 minutes or until soft. Cool. Reserve 4 pieces of rhubarb for decoration, and stir in 2 to 3 tablespoons of the sweetener.

Combine a little of the milk with the cornstarch in a small saucepan; stir in remaining milk. Cook, stirring, over medium-low heat until very thick. Remove from the heat and stir in the vanilla and 1 tablespoon of the sweetener. Fold the rhubarb into the custard and spoon into 4 individual glasses. Cover and refrigerate until chilled. Decorate with the reserved rhubarb before serving.

Makes 4 servings.

Each serving contains:

					Exchanges:	
Calories	63	Total Fat	0g	Bread	0.3
Protein	3g	Saturated Fat	0g	Fruit	1.6
Carbohydrates	12g	Cholesterol	1mg	Milk	0.2
Fiber	2g	Sodium	36mg		

Banana Cream Pie

It takes about 10 minutes to thicken the custard, so you'll need some patience. Because the meringue is made with less sugar, it will be slightly soft.

Best eaten the same day.

1	recipe Pastry for Normandy Apple Flan (page 178)
2	eggs, separated
2	tablespoons cornstarch
1	tablespoon soft margarine
1	cup nonfat milk
2	tablespoons granulated artificial sweetener or to taste
1	teaspoon vanilla extract
2	medium bananas, sliced and tossed with lemon juice
3	tablespoons sugar

Prepare pastry, chill and use to line an 8-inch tart pan. Chill 15 minutes in the refrigerator. Preheat oven to 425F (220C). Line pastry with foil, fill with dried beans, and bake 5 minutes. Remove the foil and beans and bake another 10 minutes or until golden brown.

Beat the egg yolks, cornstarch and margarine in a heatproof bowl until pale in color. Bring the milk almost to a boil in a saucepan, then gradually whisk into the egg mixture. Place the bowl over a pan of simmering water and cook, stirring constantly, until thick. Remove from the heat and allow to cool slightly. Stir in the sweetener and vanilla extract.

Arrange the banana slices in the bottom of the pastry shell, reserving a few for decoration. Pour

Each serving contains:

				Exchanges:	
Calories	244	Total Fat	11g	Bread	1.1
Protein	6g	Saturated Fat	2g	Fruit	0.7
Carbohydrates	32g	Cholesterol	54mg	Milk	0.1
Fiber	2g	Sodium	149mg	Meat	0.2
				Fat	1.9

the custard over the banana slices. Beat the egg whites until soft peaks form. Slowly beat in the sugar until stiff but not dry. Spoon the meringue over the custard, leaving the center uncovered. Bake at 300F (150C) 15 to 20 minutes or until the meringue is golden. Arrange the remaining banana slices in the center. Serve cold.

Makes 8 servings.

Light Cheesecake

A simple dessert that makes a midweek meal special. It is easy to make but looks impressive. Use chilled ingredients and serve as soon as possible; otherwise the cookies lose their crunchiness.

6	graham crackers, crushed
1	(3-oz.) pkg. fat-free cream cheese, softened
1	(8-oz.) pkg. fat-free cream cheese, softened
2	tablespoons plain fat-free yogurt
1	tablespoon granulated artificial sweetener
1/2	teaspoon vanilla extract
8	oz. raspberries, thawed if frozen
	A little granulated sweetener to taste

Put cookies in a heavy plastic bag and crush them with a rolling pin. If you buy a package of cookies and some are broken, crush them and store them in the freezer for use in desserts like this.

Divide the cracker crumbs among 4 individual glass dishes. Beat the cream cheeses, yogurt, sweetener and vanilla together in a bowl until light and fluffy. Spoon cheese mixture on top of the crumbs. Divide the raspberries among the dishes, sprinkle with a little sweetener, if desired. Serve immediately.

Makes 4 servings.

Each serving contains:

				Exchanges:	
Calories	148	Total Fat	1g	Bread	0.5
Protein	13g	Saturated Fat	0g	Fruit	1.0
Carbohydrates	20g	Cholesterol	6mg	Milk	0.1
Fiber	3g	Sodium	448mg	Fat	0.1

Apple-and-Blackberry Sponge Pudding

I don't add sugar or a sweetener to fresh fruit when making desserts, because I find that the fruit is sweet enough. However, sweetener is given as an option in the recipe. Using raspberries in place of the blackberries makes a nice variation.

1	lb. apples, peeled, cored and sliced
8	oz. blackberries, rinsed
2 to 3	tablespoons granulated artificial sweetener or to taste
5	tablespoons sugar
1/4	cup soft margarine
1/4	cup all-purpose flour
1/2	teaspoon baking powder
	Grated peel and juice of 1 lemon
1	egg, separated
1/2	cup 2% lowfat milk
2	tablespoons sliced almonds
	A little granulated artificial sweetener to serve (optional)

Preheat oven to 350F (175C). Place the apples and blackberries in the bottom of a 1-quart baking dish and sprinkle with the sweetener. Beat the sugar and margarine together in a medium bowl until creamy. Stir in the flour, baking powder, lemon peel and juice, egg yolk and milk and beat until smooth. (The mixture may look curdled.)

Plum Sponge Pudding

Replace the apple and blackberries with 1-1/2 pounds of ripe plums. Cut them in half and remove the pit before putting them in the dish. You probably will need very little, if any, sweetener.

Whisk the egg white until stiff but not dry and fold into the mixture. Spoon over the apples and black-berries to cover. Sprinkle with the almonds. Place the dish in a roasting pan and add boiling water halfway up the side of the dish.

Bake 50 minutes or until the top is golden. Dust with a little granulated sweetener before serving if desired. Serve hot.

Makes 6 servings.

Each serving contains:

					Exchanges:	
Calories	226	Total Fat	10g		Bread	0.2
Protein	3g	Saturated Fat	2g		Fruit	1.9
Carbohydrates	32g	Cholesterol	37mg		Milk	0.2
Fiber	3g	Sodium	121mg		Meat	0.2
					Fat	1.9

Pears with Raspberry Sauce

Succulent pears are enhanced with raspberries and wine.

4	medium pears
1	cup dry red wine
1 or 2	cinnamon sticks
4	whole cloves
1	tablespoon lemon juice
8	oz. raspberries, defrosted if frozen
2	tablespoons granulated artificial sweetener or to taste
	Fresh mint leaves

Peel the pears thinly, leaving stems intact. Remove the core with a knife and cut a small slice from the bottom of each so they will stand up.

Place the pears, wine, cinnamon, cloves and lemon juice in a medium saucepan over medium heat. Bring to a boil. Reduce heat, cover and simmer 15 minutes, basting and turning the pears so they will color evenly. Remove from the heat and set aside.

To make the sauce, cook the raspberries about 5 minutes over low heat or until soft. Press the raspberries through a fine strainer to remove seeds. Stir the sweetener into the raspberries. Drain the pears and mix 5 tablespoons of the wine mixture with the raspberry mixture. Pour the sauce on to serving plates and add the pears. Decorate with fresh mint.

Makes 4 servings.

Each serving contains:

				Exchanges:	
Calories	168	Total Fat	1g	Fruit	2.2
Protein	1g	Saturated Fat	0g	Fat	0.8
Carbohydrates	33g	Cholesterol	0mg		
Fiber	6g	Sodium	3mg		

Pears with Ginger Sauce

A light, low-calorie dessert that provides a clean, refreshing end to a meal.

This tastes equally delicious with a mixture of apple and pear.

Note

Fat-free cream cheese could be used to reduce the saturated fat.

4	pears, peeled, cored and thinly sliced
1	(8-oz.) pkg. light cream cheese, softened
1/4	cup fat-free plain yogurt
	Grated peel of 1 small lemon
2	teaspoons granulated artificial sweetener
2	teaspoons finely grated fresh ginger
2	tablespoons finely chopped pecans

Arrange the pear slices on four serving plates. Mix together the cream cheese, yogurt, lemon peel, sweetener and ginger. Spoon or pipe on the plates next to the pears, topped with the chopped nuts. Serve chilled.

Makes 4 servings.

Each serving contains:

Calories	262	Total Fat	13g	Fruit	1.7
Protein	8g	Saturated Fat	7g	Milk	0.4
Carbohydrates	31g	Cholesterol	32mg	Meat	0.6
Fiber	4g	Sodium	180mg	Fat	2.1

Exchanges:

Summer Fruit Layers

This dessert takes time to prepare, but the result is impressive. Don't try to rush the gelatin layers. Make sure that each layer is completely set before adding another layer. Keep the remaining gelatin mixture at room temperature until required. To frost glasses, rub the rim of the glasses with a lemon half and then dip the rims in granulated artificial sweetener.

1	(0.3-oz.) pkg. sugar-free strawberry gelatin dessert
1	cup boiling water
1	cup rosé wine
4	oz. strawberries, hulled
4	oz. blueberries
4	oz. raspberries
1	cup whipping cream

Dissolve gelatin dessert in the boiling water in a medium bowl. Cool slightly, then stir in the wine. Cool to room temperature. Reserve 2 strawberries for decoration, slice remaining strawberries and arrange in the bottom of 8 small dessert glasses. Carefully pour a layer of the gelatin mixture over the strawberries. Chill in the refrigerator until set. Repeat with a layer of blueberries and gelatin mixture and chill until set. Finally, repeat with a layer of raspberries and gelatin mixture. Chill until firm.

Whip the cream until soft peaks form. Spoon a dollop of whipped cream on each dessert. Top with a strawberry slice and serve. Serve with wafer cookies if desired.

Makes 8 servings.

Each serving contains:

				Exchanges:	
Calories	147	Total Fat	11g	Fruit	0.4
Protein	2g	Saturated Fat	7g	Milk	0.1
Carbohydrates	6g	Cholesterol	41mg	Fat	2.6
Fiber	1g	Sodium	41mg		

Spiced Apple Pie in Filo Pastry

Here is an apple pie that is low in fat and calories! Keep the fat content low by using only a small amount of melted soft margarine to brush on the pastry before baking.

1	lb. apples, peeled, cored and sliced
1/4	cup water
1/2	teaspoon ground mixed spice
1/2	teaspoon ground cinnamon
3	tablespoons golden raisins
1	tablespoon granulated artificial sweetener
1	sheet filo pastry
1	tablespoon soft margarine, melted

Preheat oven to 425F (220C). Place the apples, water and spices in a small saucepan over low heat. Cook 5 minutes, stirring occasionally, or until soft. Stir in the raisins and sweetener and spoon into a small, shallow ovenproof dish.

Brush one side of the filo pastry with the melted margarine and then tear it into pieces. Arrange the filo pastry over the apple with the buttered side up. Bake 15 minutes or until the top is golden brown. Serve warm.

Makes 4 servings.

Each serving contains:

				Exchanges:	
Calories	130	Total Fat	4g	Bread	0.2
Protein	1g	Saturated Fat	1g	Fruit	1.6
Carbohydrates	26g	Cholesterol	0mg	Fat	0.6
Fiber	3g	Sodium	50mg		

Rice Pudding with Apple and Blackberry

Substitute fresh or frozen raspberries for the blackberries if they are not in season. If you use raspberries, you may not need as much sweetener.

1/4	cup short-grain rice
2	cups nonfat milk
	Finely grated peel and juice of 1 lemon
1	vanilla bean, split open
3	tablespoons granulated artificial sweetener
12	oz. apples, peeled, cored and sliced
8	oz. blackberries
2/3	cup low-fat plain yogurt

Place the rice, milk, lemon peel and vanilla bean in a medium saucepan over medium heat. Bring to a boil. Reduce heat and simmer, uncovered, stirring occasionally, until the rice is tender and most of the milk is absorbed, 30 to 40 minutes. Turn into a large bowl and stir in 1 tablespoon of the sweetener. Let cool.

Meanwhile, place the apples and 2 tablespoons of the lemon juice in a saucepan over low heat. Cover tightly and simmer until the apples are tender and still hold their shape. Add the blackberries and cook just a few seconds. Pour the fruit into a bowl. Stir in the remaining sweetener. Cool slightly, cover and refrigerate 1 hour. Fold the yogurt into the rice, cover and refrigerate 1 hour.

Peach and Raspberry Rice

Replace the apples and blackberries with fresh peaches and raspberries or, for a winter treat, use canned peaches in natural juice and frozen raspberries and omit cooking the fruit.

Each serving contains:

Calories	161	Total Fat	1g	Bread	0.2
Protein	7g	Saturated Fat	0g	Fruit	1.4
Carbohydrates	33g	Cholesterol	3mg	Milk	0.8
Fiber	4g	Sodium	94mg		

Exchanges:

To serve, layer the apple and rice mixture in 4 individual glasses, discarding the vanilla bean. Top each with a blackberry and a slice of apple.

Makes 4 servings.

No-sugar Custard Sauce

Sweeteners should generally be added after the custard is boiled because some types lose their sweetness at high temperatures.

- 1   cup nonfat milk
- 1   tablespoon cornstarch
- 1   teaspoon vanilla extract
-     Artificial sweetener to taste

Combine a little of the milk with the cornstarch in a small saucepan; stir in remaining milk. Cook, stirring, over medium-low heat until thickened. Remove from the heat and stir in the vanilla and sweetener. Serve warm or chilled.

Makes 1 cup.

Each serving (2 ounces) contains: *Exchanges*:

Calories	31	Total Fat	0g	Bread	0.1
Protein	2g	Saturated Fat	0g	Milk	0.2
Carbohydrates	5g	Cholesterol	1mg		
Fiber	0g	Sodium	32mg		

Figs with Blackberry Sauce

A perfect fig will be unblemished and will just yield when you hold it without pressing on it. It can be any color, from pale green to purple.

When figs are not available, serve this sauce on sliced peaches or melon. This dessert makes a great presentation—try adding a couple of pretty chocolate leaves to the plate when you serve it.

8	oz. blackberries
2	tablespoons water
1	teaspoon arrowroot or cornstarch
2	teaspoons water
1 to 2	teaspoons granulated artificial sweetener, or to taste
8	ripe fresh figs

Place the blackberries and water in a small saucepan over low heat. Cook 2 to 3 minutes or until soft. Combine arrowroot or cornstarch and water. Stir mixture into the blackberries and boil, stirring, 1 minute to thicken. Press the blackberries through a fine strainer to remove seeds. Stir in the sweetener to taste.

Cut off the fig stems. From the stem end, make 2 right-angle cuts, three-quarters of the way through. Open to resemble flowers. Place 2 figs on each of 4 serving plates. Spoon a little blackberry sauce over each fig. Serve the remaining sauce separately.

Makes 4 servings.

Each serving contains:

Calories	106	Total Fat	1g	*Exchanges:*	
Protein	1g	Saturated Fat	0g	Fruit	1.5
Carbohydrates	27g	Cholesterol	0mg		
Fiber	6g	Sodium	1mg		

Nectarine-and-Raspberry Dessert

For a special finish, rub the rim of the sundae dish or goblet glass with a lemon half and then coat with a granulated artificial sweetener before filling.

2	ripe nectarines
5	oz. raspberries, fresh or frozen
1	(8-oz.) pkg. light cream cheese, softened
3/4	cup fat-free, sugar-free raspberry yogurt
3	tablespoons granulated artificial sweetener or to taste
	Mint leaves to decorate

Halve and remove seeds from the nectarines. Place in a blender or food processor and purée until smooth. Add a little sweetener to taste and set aside. Reserving 4 raspberries for decoration, purée the remaining raspberries until smooth and strain to remove the seeds, if desired. Pour into the bottom of four sundae dishes. Stir the cheese and yogurt together, and add a little sweetener to taste.

Layer the yogurt mixture and nectarine purée in the sundae dishes, finishing with a layer of yogurt mixture. Chill before serving, decorated with the reserved raspberries and mint leaves.

Makes 4 servings.

Each serving contains:				*Exchanges*:	
Calories	262	Total Fat	10g	Fruit	0.8
Protein	11g	Saturated Fat	6g	Milk	0.3
Carbohydrates	32g	Cholesterol	34mg	Meat	0.6
Fiber	2g	Sodium	220mg	Fat	1.7

Chilled Lemon Soufflé

I remember making my first lemon soufflé during my home-economics class. It makes a refreshing dessert to end a dinner party.

Note

Raw eggs, and dishes containing them, are unsuitable for older adults, young children or pregnant women.

Grated peel and juice of 3 lemons
6   eggs, separated
5   tablespoons granulated artificial sweetener
2   tablespoons unflavored gelatin powder
1-1/2   cups whipping cream
1/4   cup chopped mixed nuts, toasted
Shreds of lemon peel to decorate

Tie a double strip of waxed paper around a 1-quart soufflé dish to make a 3-inch collar. Lightly brush the inside of the paper with a little oil. Set aside.

With an electric mixer, beat the lemon peel, egg yolks and sweetener together in a bowl until pale. Pour 7 tablespoons of the lemon juice into a small saucepan, sprinkle in the gelatin and let soak 5 minutes to soften. Place over low heat and stir until the gelatin dissolves. Cool slightly, then stir into the egg-yolk mixture.

Whip the cream in a medium bowl until it forms soft peaks. Reserving a little for piping, fold the remaining cream into the egg-yolk mixture.

Beat the egg whites in a large bowl until stiff but not dry. With a large spatula, carefully fold egg whites into the egg-yolk mixture. Gently pour the mixture into the prepared soufflé dish. Refrigerate at least 4 hours or until set.

Each serving contains:

				Exchanges:	
Calories	321	Total Fat	30g	Bread	0.4
Protein	10g	Saturated Fat	16g	Fruit	1.8
Carbohydrates	4g	Cholesterol	294mg	Milk	0.5
Fiber	1g	Sodium	91mg		

Carefully ease the paper collar away from the soufflé with a knife dipped in hot water. Press the toasted nuts around the edge of the soufflé with a small metal spatula. Decorate the top with whipped-cream rosettes and the lemon peel. Serve as soon as possible.

Makes 6 to 8 servings.

Peach Yogurt Crunch

A simple dessert that children can easily make themselves, with the help of an adult to purée the peaches. Substitute other canned fruit, such as apricots or pears for a variation.

1	(14-oz.) can peach slices in natural juice
3	tablespoons granulated artificial sweetener, or to taste
1	pint fat-free frozen vanilla yogurt
4	graham crackers

Drain the peaches, reserving the juice. Place the peaches and 2 tablespoons of the juice in a blender or food processor and blend to a smooth purée. Stir in 2 tablespoons of sweetener or to taste. Layer the peach purée and yogurt in 4 or 5 glasses. Crumble the graham crackers over the top and serve.

Make 4 or 5 servings.

Each serving contains:				Exchanges:	
Calories	169	Total Fat	1g	Bread	0.4
Protein	6g	Saturated Fat	0g	Fruit	1.8
Carbohydrates	36g	Cholesterol	2mg	Milk	0.5
Fiber	2g	Sodium	111mg		

Frozen Orange Cups

I find it easier to scoop out the pulp if I use a grapefruit knife to score around the outside and then a spoon to scoop it out. This dessert is particularly refreshing in the summer months.

4	large oranges
1-1/4	cups low-fat plain yogurt
1	(8-oz.) carton fat-free cream cheese, softened
1/4	cup granulated artificial sweetener
	Sprigs of fresh mint to decorate

Trim a small amount from the bottom of each orange so that they stand upright. Cut away the stem ends and set aside. Scoop out the pulp and place in a food processor or blender with the yogurt and cream cheese. Add the sweetener and process 10 to 20 seconds or until smooth. Pass through a sieve if desired. Pour into a freezerproof container. Freeze the orange cups and the orange mixture 4 hours, mashing the frozen mixture with a fork after 2 hours to remove ice crystals. (Or, process the mixture in the food processor or blender). Remove the ice cream from the freezer 10 minutes before serving. Serve in scoops in the orange cups. Decorate with mint.

Makes 4 servings.

Each serving contains:

Calories	156	Total Fat	0g	Fruit	1.0
Protein	14g	Saturated Fat	0g	Milk	0.5
Carbohydrates	25g	Cholesterol	6mg		
Fiber	2g	Sodium	333mg		

Exchanges:

Bread Pudding

This is a delicious way to use up bread that is no longer perfectly fresh!

I used an artificial sweetener to replace the sugar in this recipe. If you prefer, you can use 1/3 cup sugar instead.

3	cups cubed day-old bread
1/2	cup raisins
1	small carrot, peeled and finely grated
2	tablespoons granulated artificial sweetener
1-1/2	cups nonfat milk, warmed
1	egg, beaten
1/2	teaspoon grated nutmeg
1	teaspoon vanilla extract

Preheat oven to 350F (175C). Grease a 1-1/2-quart casserole dish. Place the bread in the casserole dish and sprinkle the sweetener, raisins and carrot over the bread. Beat the milk, egg, nutmeg and vanilla together and pour over the bread. Let soak 15 minutes.

Bake about 45 minutes or until golden brown. Cool in the dish.

Makes 6 servings.

Each serving contains:

				Exchanges:	
Calories	143	Total Fat	2g	Bread	0.7
Protein	5g	Saturated Fat	1g	Vegetable	0.2
Carbohydrates	26g	Cholesterol	37mg	Fruit	0.7
Fiber	2g	Sodium	153mg	Milk	0.2
				Meat	0.2
				Fat	0.1

Lemon-and-Lime Meringue Pie

A variation of a family favorite. Lemon and lime together deliver a rich citrus flavor.

Note

Due to the reduced sugar content, this meringue topping will have a slightly softer texture than most.

1	recipe Pastry for Normandy Apple Flan (page 178)
	Finely grated peel and juice of 1 small lemon
	Finely grated peel and juice of 1 small lime
1	tablespoon soft margarine
3	tablespoons cornstarch
2	eggs, separated
1	tablespoon granulated artificial sweetener
	or to taste
2	tablespoons sugar

Prepare pastry, chill and use to line an 8-inch tart pan. Chill 15 minutes in the refrigerator. Preheat oven to 425F (220C). Line pastry with foil, fill with dried beans, and bake 5 minutes. Remove the foil and beans and bake another 10 minutes.

Reduce the oven temperature to 300F (150C).

Meanwhile, prepare the filling. Pour the lemon and lime juices into a 1-cup measure. Add cold water to make 1 cup. Combine a little of the juice with the cornstarch in a small saucepan; stir in remaining juice and margarine. Bring to a boil. Reduce heat and cook, stirring, over medium-low heat until thickened. Beat a little of lemon mixture into the egg yolks. Return to saucepan and cook, stirring, 1 minute. Cool slightly and add the sweetener to taste. Pour into the pastry shell.

Each serving contains:				*Exchanges:*	
Calories	203	Total Fat	11g	Bread	1.2
Protein	4g	Saturated Fat	2g	Fruit	0.2
Carbohydrates	23g	Cholesterol	53mg	Meat	0.2
Fiber	2g	Sodium	133mg	Fat	1.9

Beat the egg whites until soft peaks form. Gradually beat in the sugar until stiff but not dry. Spoon the meringue over the filling.

Bake 20 to 25 minutes or until golden brown. Serve warm or cold.

Makes 8 servings.

Strawberry Milkshake

Make sure that the milk is ice-cold before you make the milkshake so that it can be served while it is frothy. Add a little artificial sweetener if you like to give a sweeter taste.

- 6 oz. fresh strawberries, hulled
- 1 (6-oz.) carton fat-free strawberry yogurt
- 2 cups nonfat milk

Place all the ingredients in a blender and process for a few seconds until smooth and frothy. Pour into tall glasses and serve.

Makes 4 servings.

Peach Melba Shake

Use a large ripe peach and a carton of raspberry yogurt.

Each serving contains:				*Exchanges:*	
Calories	102	Total Fat	1g	Fruit	0.2
Protein	6g	Saturated Fat	0g	Milk	0.5
Carbohydrates	18g	Cholesterol	5mg		
Fiber	1g	Sodium	84mg		

Raspberry Ice

An economical dessert! Vary the flavor by using other soft fruits, such as strawberries or blueberries. If you prefer a sweeter taste, 2 to 3 tablespoons of artificial sweetener may be added with the fruit.

    1   (14-oz.) can evaporated milk, chilled overnight
    12 oz. fresh raspberries

Using an electric mixer, beat the evaporated milk in a chilled bowl until thick and creamy and doubled in volume. Purée the raspberries using a blender or food processor and strain to remove the seeds. Fold into the evaporated milk until evenly mixed. Turn into a freezerproof container. Cover and freeze 1 hour or until mixture starts to freeze around the edges. Whisk well, then return to freezer until firm. Remove from the freezer and place in the refrigerator 30 minutes before serving to soften. Serve in scoops with fresh fruit.

Makes 8 servings.

Each serving contains:				Exchanges:	
Calories	87	Total Fat	4g	Fruit	0.3
Protein	4g	Saturated Fat	2g	Milk	0.4
Carbohydrates	10g	Cholesterol	15mg	Fat	0.7
Fiber	2g	Sodium	53mg		

Tiramisù

This delicious dessert is a favorite in Italian restaurants, but my recipe has fewer calories!

Tirami Sù, *as the Italians would write it, literally means "pick me up." If you like the creamy dessert but don't like coffee, make a chocolate version instead. Use a chocolate liqueur and replace the strong coffee with a low-calorie chocolate drink.*

1   egg, separated
2   tablespoons granulated artificial sweetener
1/2 teaspoon vanilla extract
3   (3-oz.) pkgs. fat-free cream cheese, softened
1/2 cup strong black coffee
2   tablespoons coffee liqueur
1/2 Yellow Cake layer (page 133)
1/2 teaspoon cocoa powder

Place the egg yolk, sweetener, vanilla extract and cream cheese in a bowl and beat to a smooth consistency. Whisk the egg white until stiff and gently fold into the cream-cheese mixture with a spatula. Mix the coffee and liqueur together in a bowl. Cut the cake into 1-inch strips and dip into the coffee and liqueur until it absorbs the mixture, but not until it falls apart.

Layer half the cake in the bottom of 4 individual glass dishes or 1 medium serving dish, cutting into smaller pieces to fit. Cover with half the cheese mixture. Top with remaining cake and finish with a layer of cheese mixture. Dust with cocoa powder and refrigerate at least 1 hour before serving.

Makes 4 servings.

Each serving contains:

					Exchanges:
Calories	241	Total Fat	8g	Bread	0.5
Protein	13g	Saturated Fat	2g	Fruit	0.8
Carbohydrates	25g	Cholesterol	85mg	Meat	0.4
Fiber	0g	Sodium	469mg	Fat	1.6

Clafouti

Clafouti is a French dessert that I've adapted.
I make this recipe when cherries are in season;
otherwise the dish can be rather expensive.

This dish is super made with pitted plums or prunes in place of the cherries.

3	tablespoons all-purpose flour
	Pinch of salt
3	eggs, beaten
2	tablespoons sugar
1-1/2	cups milk
12	oz. fresh red cherries, pitted
2	tablespoons soft margarine
2	tablespoons granulated artificial sweetener

Preheat oven to 425F (220C). Sift together the flour and salt into a bowl, then beat in the eggs and sugar. Heat the milk until almost boiling and beat into the egg mixture.

Lightly grease a large, shallow ovenproof dish and arrange the cherries over the bottom. Pour the batter over the top and dot with the margarine.

Bake 20 to 25 minutes until the custard is set and golden brown. Sprinkle with the sweetener to taste and serve warm.

Makes 8 servings.

Each serving contains:

						Exchanges:	
Calories	129		Total Fat	6g		Bread	0.1
Protein	5g		Saturated Fat	2g		Fruit	0.6
Carbohydrates	15g		Cholesterol	83mg		Milk	0.2
Fiber	1g		Sodium	106mg		Meat	0.4
						Fat	0.9

Holiday Cooking

Holidays are meant to be enjoyed, so try to make everything as normal as possible for you and your family. With care and advance planning, you can enjoy the holidays the same as always and stay in control of your diabetes. This chapter includes recipes for many traditional holiday foods. The whole family will like these dishes.

Cranberry Sauce

Fresh cranberries are usually available in supermarkets just before Thanksgiving. Buy several packages and freeze until needed. Keep the sugar content low by using an artificial sweetener to sweeten the sauce.

This sauce will not keep in a jar the way a high-sugar version will, but it does freeze well. Thaw thoroughly before serving.

1	(12-oz.) pkg. fresh cranberries, picked over and rinsed
	Grated peel and juice of 1 orange
5	tablespoons water
2	to 3 tablespoons granulated artificial sweetener or to taste

Place the cranberries, orange peel, orange juice and water in a saucepan over low heat. Simmer 15 minutes or until the berries are tender. Remove from the heat and add the sweetener to taste.

Makes 6 to 8 servings.

Each serving contains:

				Exchanges:	
Calories	28	Total Fat	0g	Fruit	0.6
Protein	0g	Saturated Fat	0g		
Carbohydrates	7g	Cholesterol	0mg		
Fiber	2g	Sodium	1mg		

Roast Rock Cornish Hens

Many people like to serve individual Rock Cornish hens at Christmas instead of turkey, particularly if the number of guests is small.

2	tablespoons olive oil
1	lemon, sliced
	Sprigs of thyme
	Bay leaves
4	Rock Cornish hens, thawed and rinsed
1	tablespoon all-purpose flour
1	cup chicken broth
	Salt and freshly ground black pepper

Preheat oven to 325F (165C). Heat the oil in a large Dutch oven over medium heat. Place lemon slices, thyme and bay leaves in the cavity of each hen. Add the hens and cook, turning often, until browned.

Cover and bake 1-1/2 hours or until the hens are tender. Place the hens on a heated serving dish and keep hot. Meanwhile, skim the fat from the cooking juices. Stir in the flour and gradually add the stock. Boil, stirring constantly, 2 to 3 minutes and season with salt. Remove lemon slices and herbs before serving. Serve the gravy with the hens. Serve with wild rice and green vegetables.

Makes 4 servings.

Each serving contains:				*Exchanges:*	
Calories	804	Total Fat	48g	Bread	0.1
Protein	84g	Saturated Fat	13g	Meat	12.2
Carbohydrates	2g	Cholesterol	268mg	Fat	2.2
Fiber	0g	Sodium	1284mg		

Peppered Roast Beef

Roast beef is ideal to serve on Christmas Day instead of turkey. The spicy coating gives the beef a rich flavor.

1	(3-1/2 lb.) lean beef roast, such as eye of round
3	tablespoons crushed mixed peppercorns
6	tablespoons prepared horseradish sauce
2	tablespoons all-purpose flour
2	tablespoons cold water
2	cups beef stock
	Salt and freshly ground black pepper

Preheat oven to 425F (220C). Trim the beef of any excess fat and pat dry with paper towels. Mix the peppercorns and horseradish sauce together to form a paste. Spread the paste over the meat and place on a rack set in a roasting pan. Cover and cook 15 minutes per pound, plus 15 minutes, for rare, 20 minutes per pound, plus 20 minutes, for medium, and 25 minutes per pound, plus 25 minutes, for well done.

Remove the roast from the oven and let stand, covered, on a warmed platter about 10 minutes before carving.

While the roast stands, drain the excess fat from the roasting pan. Mix the flour with the cold water to form a smooth paste. Stir the paste into the pan juices with the stock. Bring to a boil. Reduce heat and simmer, stirring constantly until the gravy is thickened. Season with salt and pepper.

Serve the roast beef with potatoes, the gravy and green vegetables.

Makes 8 servings.

Traditional Sunday Dinner

Leek and Cheese Soup (page 27)

Peppered Roast Beef (opposite)

Dry-roasted Potatoes (page 182), carrots and a green vegetable

Spiced Apple-and-Almond Cake (page138)

Each serving contains:

Calories	386	Total Fat	14g	Bread	0.1
Protein	59g	Saturated Fat	6g	Vegetable	0.1
Carbohydrates	2g	Cholesterol	141mg	Meat	6.9
Fiber	0g	Sodium	238mg	Fat	0.4

Exchanges:

Creamy Fruit Dessert

This is an easy dessert to make, yet looks impressive if set in a decorative jelly mold and decorated with fresh summer fruits. I like to serve this with strawberries, raspberries, red currants and black currants, grown in my mother's garden and full of flavor. These fruits have very little carbohydrate and do not need to be counted as part of a carbohydrate allowance.

1	cup boiling water
1	(0.3-oz.) pkg. sugar-free raspberry gelatin dessert
1	(8-oz.) pkg. frozen mixed fruits or raspberries
1	(1.3-oz.) pkg. whipped topping
1/2	cup nonfat milk
2/3	cup raspberry-flavored fat-free yogurt

Pour the boiling water into a medium bowl, add the gelatin dessert mix and stir to dissolve. Stir the frozen fruit into the gelatin mixture.

Prepare whipped topping with the milk according to package instructions. Fold in the yogurt. Fold the yogurt mixture into the gelatin mixture. Cover and refrigerate 2 or 3 hours or until set.

Makes 6 servings.

Each serving contains:

Calories	110	Total Fat	3g	Bread	0.2
Protein	4g	Saturated Fat	2g	Fruit	0.7
Carbohydrates	19g	Cholesterol	1mg	Milk	0.1
Fiber	1g	Sodium	70mg	Fat	0.5

Exchanges:

Normandy Apple Flan

Even though I adapted this dessert from the original, reducing the fat and calories, it is still rather high in both quantities for an everyday meal. However, it does make a nice dessert when entertaining or as an occasional treat. It is best served warm.

Pastry
3/4	cup all-purpose flour
3/4	cup whole-wheat flour
	Pinch of salt
1/3	cup soft margarine
2	to 3 tablespoons cold water

Filling
1/4	cup soft margarine
2	tablespoons granulated artificial sweetener
2	eggs
2	tablespoons cornstarch
4	oz. ground almonds
1/4	teaspoon almond extract
1-1/4	lb. apples
2	tablespoons reduced-sugar apricot jam
2	tablespoons water

Prepare the pastry: Sift the flours and salt into a bowl. Add any bran remaining in the sifter back into the bowl. Cut in the margarine until the mixture resembles fine bread crumbs. Add enough cold water to mix to a soft dough. Shape into a ball, cover and refrigerate 30 minutes.

Preheat oven to 400F (205C). Roll out dough on a lightly floured board to an 11-inch circle. Use to line a 9-inch tart pan. Line pastry with foil and add about 1-1/2 cups dried beans. Bake 10 minutes. Remove the beans and foil and bake 5 minutes. Remove from oven.

Prepare the filling: Beat the margarine with the sweetener. Beat in the eggs, cornstarch, ground almonds and almond extract. Spread the almond mixture over the cooled pastry shell. Peel, core and thinly slice the apples. Arrange over the almond mixture. Bake 8 minutes. Reduce the heat to 350F (175C) and cook another 15 to 20 minutes or until golden.

Melt the apricot jam and water together in a small saucepan. Remove the tart from the pan and brush with the apricot glaze. Serve warm.

Makes 10 servings.

Each serving contains:				*Exchanges*:	
Calories	288	Total Fat	18g	Bread	0.9
Protein	6g	Saturated Fat	3g	Fruit	0.9
Carbohydrates	28g	Cholesterol	43mg	Meat	0.5
Fiber	4g	Sodium	140mg	Fat	3.1

Raspberry Trifle

A mixture of summer fruits may be used in place of the raspberries. For a burst of summer in the middle of winter, I use frozen mixed berries.

1/2	(1-lb.) pkg. frozen raspberries without sugar, thawed and drained
1	(0.3-oz.) pkg. sugar-free raspberry gelatin dessert
2	tablespoons all-purpose flour
1	cup nonfat milk
1	teaspoon vanilla extract
2	tablespoons granulated artificial sweetener, or to taste
1/2	cup whipping cream, whipped, or reduced-fat whipped topping

Place the fruit in the bottom of a glass serving bowl. Prepare the gelatin dessert mix according to the directions on the package. Pour over the raspberries and place in the refrigerator to set.

Combine flour and 2 tablespoons milk to a paste in a saucepan. Whisk in remaining milk. Cook, stirring constantly, over medium heat until thickened. Remove from the heat and add vanilla and artificial sweetener to taste. Allow to cool before pouring over the gelatin. Spread the whipped cream over the custard, cover and refrigerate until chilled.

Makes 6 to 8 servings.

Each serving contains: *Exchanges:*

Calories	108	Total Fat	6g	Bread	0.1
Protein	3g	Saturated Fat	4g	Fruit	0.4
Carbohydrates	10g	Cholesterol	23mg	Milk	0.2
Fiber	2g	Sodium	64mg	Fat	1.3

Mince Tarts

Use a small star or holly cutter to decorate the mince tarts. I always make my pastry in a food processor, which gives a shorter texture and makes handling easier. You can buy reduced-sugar mincemeat in some supermarkets, but why not try my easy recipe on page 184?

	Pastry (for Normandy Apple Flan, page 178)
1/4	cup Meatless Mincemeat (page 184)
	or other mincemeat
	Milk for glazing
	Granulated artificial sweetener (optional)

Prepare and chill the pastry as directed on page 178.

Preheat oven to 400F (205C). Roll out pastry on a lightly floured board. Using a 2-1/2-inch-round cutter and a small star cutter, cut out an equal number of rounds and stars.

Place the pastry rounds in mini muffin cups or small tart pans. Add 1 teaspoon of mincemeat to each. Place a star on mincemeat in each tart. Bake 10 to 15 minutes or until crust is golden brown. Brush with a little milk and sprinkle with a little sweetener, if desired, when the pies come out of the oven. Serve warm.

Makes 12 to 16 tarts.

Each serving contains:

				Exchanges:	
Calories	111	Total Fat	5g	Bread	0.7
Protein	2g	Saturated Fat	1g	Fruit	0.1
Carbohydrates	14g	Cholesterol	0mg	Fat	1.0
Fiber	1g	Sodium	72mg		

Dry-roasted Potatoes

Roast potatoes without the fat! These potatoes are a mini version of baked potatoes, with a crunchy outside and soft potato in the center. They are best served with a roast dinner with gravy; otherwise, they may seem rather dry.

2-1/2	lb. Russet potatoes, peeled and halved
	Salt
2	teaspoons ground paprika

Preheat oven to 425F (220C). Cook the potatoes in lightly salted boiling water 10 minutes. Drain well and turn into a roasting pan. Sprinkle the paprika over the potatoes and mix well to coat. Roast on the bottom rack 1 hour and 10 minutes, turning several times during cooking, or until tender.

Serves 6.

Each serving contains:

Calories	176	Total Fat	0g	Bread	2.5
Protein	4g	Saturated Fat	0g		
Carbohydrates	41g	Cholesterol	0mg		
Fiber	3g	Sodium	98mg		

Exchanges:

Frozen Fruit Bombe

This dessert makes a delicious, refreshing alternative to a rich dessert.

Suitable for freezing. Cool and pack into a rigid freezer container. Freeze up to three months. Thaw and then warm in a hot oven 3 to 4 minutes before serving.

1	(1/4-oz.) pkg. unflavored gelatin
1/2	cup water
1	(6-oz.) can evaporated milk, chilled overnight
1	(8-oz.) carton fat-free cream cheese, softened
1	tablespoon granulated artificial sweetener
3/4	cup dark raisins
2	tablespoons brandy
1/4	cup slivered almonds

Combine gelatin and water in a small saucepan. Let stand 5 minutes to soften gelatin. Heat over low heat, stirring, until gelatin dissolves. Set aside to cool. Whisk the evaporated milk in a chilled bowl until doubled in size and stiff peaks form. Fold the cooled gelatin into the evaporated milk together with the cheese and sweetener. Place in a shallow tray and freeze 1 hour or until partially set. Meanwhile, soak the raisins in the brandy.

Turn milk mixture into a bowl and whisk thoroughly. Stir in the almonds and soaked raisins. Place in a lightly greased 1-quart metal bowl. Freeze overnight or until solid. Remove from the freezer 5 minutes before serving. Turn out on to a serving plate and serve immediately.

Makes 6 servings.

Each serving contains:

				Exchanges:	
Calories	170	Total Fat	4g	Fruit	1.1
Protein	11g	Saturated Fat	1g	Milk	0.3
Carbohydrates	23g	Cholesterol	5mg	Meat	0.2
Fiber	1g	Sodium	221mg	Fat	0.7

Meatless Mincemeat

Making your own mincemeat means that you can cut down on the sugar content considerably. This recipe has a natural sweetness from just the dried fruit and fruit juice. However, it will need to be used within one week or frozen in a plastic container for up to 3 months.

8	oz. raisins
8	oz. golden raisins
4	oz. dried apricots, finely chopped
4	oz. glacé cherries, rinsed, dried and finely chopped
2	oz. chopped mixed nuts
1	large carrot, peeled and finely grated
	Finely grated peel and juice of 1 lemon
1/4	cup unsweetened orange juice
1	tablespoon brandy or rum (optional)

Mix all the ingredients together in a large bowl. Cover and refrigerate 2 days, stirring occasionally.

Use as desired or pack into clean, sterilized jars and refrigerate up to 1 week or freeze in plastic containers up to 3 months.

Makes about 2 pounds.

Each serving (3 ounces) contains:				Exchanges:	
Calories	239	Total Fat	3g	Vegetable	0.1
Protein	3g	Saturated Fat	0g	Fruit	2.8
Carbohydrates	55g	Cholesterol	0mg	Meat	0.1
Fiber	3g	Sodium	10mg	Fat	0.5

Index